MW01277951

WHAT'S IN A NAME?

ENCOURAGEMENT FOR GOD'S DAUGHTERS

SHEILA ROBERTS

PUBLISHED BY ROBERTS INK PRESS

OTHER NON-FICTION BOOKS BY
SHEILA ROBERTS

Old is not a Four-Letter Word

Unexpected Journey

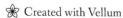

ACKNOWLEDGMENTS

I would like toi thank Becky Gorton and Jessica Errico for their helpful input and editorial comments. And thank you to the many women who graciously let me share their stories in this book.

CONTENTS

ONE
WHAT'S IN A NAME?

You probably know who thought up that question. It was William Shakespeare. He didn't seem to think names were all that important. After all, no matter what you call it, a rose still smells like a rose, right?

I would beg to differ with old Will. What if I told you I was sending you a lovely bouquet of used toilet paper. Bet you wouldn't be waiting by the door for that. Names define things. They provide us labels for visual images. Names not only help us keep track of all those people who come in and out of our lives, they also are packed with meaning and memories, innuendo, pride and hurt. Names are powerful. If they weren't, we wouldn't pore over baby name books when we're expecting. And we certainly wouldn't call each other names when we're angry.

God, Himself, showed us the importance of names when He called the light day and the darkness night.[1] He named the first human He created, giving him the name Adam, which means of the soil.[2] A good reminder for Adam of his origins.

Adam the earth creature was allowed to name the other

animals that God had created (which makes perfect sense as he could hardly refer to them all as Hey, You). Then came the first woman, who Adam was also allowed to name. He chose that name because it signified something important to him. He and this woman shared the same DNA. "This is now bone of my bone and flesh of my flesh."[3]

Eve got her chance to bestow a name with the birth of her first son, Cain. "...She said, 'With the help of the Lord I have brought forth a man.'"[4] Look at the significance of that. I can only imagine her wonder at this living creature that had come out of her. The name she picked acknowledged the wonder of it all and the part God played in getting the human race started.

But what do you think when you hear the name Cain, especially when you pair it with the name Abel, the brother he killed? It probably isn't wow, first baby born to the new human race.

For better or for worse, names often become inextricably linked with certain people, both real and fictional and those names can produce a visceral reaction. For example, what do you think of when you hear the name Freddy Kruger? If you are aware of the popular *Nightmare on Elm Street* film series from the nineteen-eighties and early nineties, you think horror. Same with the name Dracula.

I'm guessing you wouldn't pick any of the following names for your child.

Scrooge

The name Scrooge has become synonymous with stinginess thanks to Dickens's famous tale, *A Christmas Carol*, which introduced us to the bitter old miser, Ebeneezer Scrooge. If you wanted to guilt someone into parting with his money, you would scold, "Don't be such a Scrooge," and that person would know you weren't offering a compliment. Now, thanks to Dr. Seuss, we have a more modern version of Ebeneezer – the

Grinch. Here in the U.S., along with most of the western world, if you call someone a Grinch everyone knows who you're talking about and what you mean.

Adolf

Do you know anyone who named their child Adolf? Unless you're a neo-Nazi, that name is no longer one to bestow with pride on a child. Why? Because we associate it with the infamous dictator of World War II. If you were to name your child after him, people would question your values.

Benedict.

Thanks to a popular English actor of the same name, this could become fashionable in the U.S. But certainly, after the Revolutionary War, no one was naming little Junior Benedict... unless the parents lived in England! On our side of the pond Benedict Arnold was considered a traitor, and to name a son after him would have been considered a sure sign that you were a traitor also.

Judas.

Uh, no. Not for a Christian anyway.

Jezebel.

In Christian circles this is not a name bestowed on a daughter because the Jezebel we've read about in the Bible was, to put it mildly, a horrible person. In our grandmothers' time, if someone called a woman a Jezebel everyone knew she wasn't bestowing a compliment.

Delilah.

Great name if you're going to be cutting hair for a living. Again, this is not a name we expect to fine in the Christian community because of the negative overtones.

Here are some other interesting names I've actually seen: Dr. Rencher (a dentist), Dr. Frankenstein. This is pronounced Frankensteen, but I wouldn't know that if I was searching online for a new doctor and, even though he's probably great, I can't help wondering how much business he loses because of his name. Or how about Dr. Bonebreak? (Oh, my!) Then there are the sisters I read about, Ima Hogg and Ura Hogg. These sisters successfully sued their parents. Good for you, girls!

On the other hand, what do you think of when you hear these names? Joshua, Mary, Theresa, Luke. We favor these names because they are associated with godly people.

We often associate names with people we've known. Ever hear someone say, "I can't stand that name. I knew a _____ once." (Fill in the blank.) Or, "I'd never name my kid after _____." (Again, fill in the blank.) The undesirable name is usually associated with someone who was hurtful to the person in some way or whose behavior was nothing to emulate. On the other hand, we name our children after parents, best friends, loved ones, people we admire because we want to honor those people.

We often give our children names we hope they'll live up to, hence the popularity of beloved biblical names. Who wouldn't want her daughter to have the godly character of Mary? Who wouldn't want his son to be a rock like Peter or stalwart and loved like John? And then there's the ultimate tribute of naming a son Jesus, something that has, in the past, been especially popular in countries like Spain and Mexico.

When picking names for our children, we also gravitate toward ones with encouraging meanings or happy or noble associations. My grandmother named one of my uncles after a famous evangelist in our family line. One of my sweetest friends is named Faith. The way she chooses to live her life matches up to her name.

Hearing some names makes us smile or tear up while hearing other names makes us cringe. Names and character go hand in hand, as do names and self-worth. Which is why there is no truth to that old bit of armor we all have put up as children: Sticks and stones may break my bones, but words will never hurt me. Oh, yes, they will.

The names we're given, the names we're called – they all influence us. We may be inspired to live up to the name we were given, or we may struggle to live down a bad nickname we've earned. Or one we haven't! Often, we wind up focusing on a name that, as children of God, no longer belongs to us.

Why do we do that? We do it because what we are told about ourselves, whether good or bad, has a habit of burrowing into our souls. Yep, names matter.

The ones that matter most of all are the ones God gives us. Those are encouraging and filled with hope.

It took many years for the concept of the power and influence of names to sink into my mind and heart in a way that I really could comprehend it and let go of some of the negative ones I'd adopted. I hope as we talk about the importance of the names God bestows on us that you will also reject those negative names you might have taken on and that you will come to a deeper understanding of your relationship with your heavenly Father. I hope that you will come to see the beauty in the name He has given you, that you will grow into it and walk in it, and enjoy the healing, freedom and blessing that comes with knowing who you are and Whose you are.

Let's delve deeper into the significance of names and see what we can discover about our God and ourselves.

1. Genesis 1:5
2. Genesis 5:2, King James translation
3. Genesis 2:23, King James translation
4. Genesis 4:1b

TWO
THE NAMES OF GOD

Before we can even begin to discuss ourselves and the names we give each other, both good and bad, we need to talk about the many names of God because all things begin with Him.

When we call someone a name, we're making a statement about that person's character. When we name a child, we are often making a statement about what we hope that child's character will become. The names we give God are an attempt to understand the infinite Being who created us, to try and to get a handle on who this Being is, what He requires and how our relationship with Him works. When we study the Bible, we see that the names people have given to God after an encounter with His revelation of His character to them. These names are hugely important, for in knowing His character we can come to appreciate, honor, and trust Him to work in, for and through us. Our names, our understanding of who we are, is tied directly to Him and who He is.

We see God called by many names throughout the Bible (over one hundred). This Being is so complex and multi-faceted that as we read the accounts of His interaction with humanity in the Bible, we can understand why so many names have been given Him. All in an attempt to describe Who He is. Each person would see a glimpse and say, "Ah, that is who He is." And they would be right. That was who He is ... and so much more. I'm sure that even with an eternity to spend in His presence we will never be able to fully comprehend our Creator's greatness.

But there are certain things we can know about Him thanks to the written Word. So, let's spend some time talking about those aspects of His character and some of His names.

El

This simply means The Strong One. It can also be translated as God. Moses calls him that in Exodus 15:2, after the Israelites successfully fled from the Egyptians across a miraculously dry seabed. Moses says, "I will sing to the Lord, for he is highly exalted." This is the New International Version translation, but the original word for Lord here was El.

Our God is strong. He is many other things as well, so we see El paired with other titles.

El Elyon

This name means Most High, Exalted. We first see it used in Genesis 14:18, a very interesting Old Testament passage where Abram (aka Abraham), the father of the Jewish nation – we'll talk more about him and his two names later – meets a mysterious priest named Melchizedek. Abram had returned from rescuing his nephew Lot, who was living in the suburbs of Sodom and had gotten caught in the middle of a war between local kings. After routing the enemy, Abram returned a hero and was greeted by the king of Sodom. He was also greeted by Melchizedek, priest of ... wait for it ... El Elyon, God Most High.

In a time when everything and every place had a god, this

was saying something. This God was not just *a* god, He was *the* God, the highest of them all. That is the God we serve.

El Shaddai

We already know that El means God, the Strong One. Shaddai, which is believed to come from Shad, means breast in Hebrew. Coupled together these words show us the mighty, caring power of a God who nourishes and supplies the needs of His people.

El Roi

This means The God Who Sees. He was given that name by a servant woman. If you go to Genesis 16, you'll find the story of Hagar, who was the servant of Sarai, Abram's wife. Hagar is the first recorded surrogate mother in history.

God had promised Abram and Sarai a child, but it wasn't looking good as Sarai was long past menopause. She got the idea that maybe, just maybe, God wanted some help with His plan. She presented her Egyptian servant, Hagar, to Abram. *Get her pregnant, but I'll be right there at the birth and that will make me the legitimate mother.*

The plan worked. Hagar became pregnant. And cocky. And soon all was not well in the household of Abram. We're told that Sarai mistreated her maid. (Dealt harshly, abused – pick your translation, but none of them sound like it was good for Hagar).

Hagar finally ran away into the desert and wound up camping out at a spring, wondering what to do next. It was there the angel of the LORD found her and told her all would be well.

One minute she was alone, facing starvation and death, the next a man appeared out of nowhere, telling her it would be okay. Hagar knew she had experienced a divine encounter of some sort with God. He had seen her unhappiness and comforted her, and she named Him The God Who Sees.[1]

El Olam

This means The Eternal God, The Everlasting God. We see it used in Genesis 21:33, when Abram, a stranger in a strange land, called on that name. We see it in Isaiah 40:28, where the Old Testament prophet Isaiah says, "Do you not know? Have you not heard? The LORD is the everlasting God, the Creator of the ends of the earth."[2]

I love this. Isaiah is basically saying, "Where have you people been? This is common knowledge. Our God is indestructible and infinite. He will always be with us."

This is comforting knowledge. This God of all gods is not constrained by the limits of time. He is eternal and won't expire or vanish. He is the only constant in the universe and in our lives. Kingdoms crumble, governments collapse, but God's kingdom remains forever. He's not going anywhere, which means we can count on Him from generation to generation.

Yahweh (Jehovah)

In Hebrew text this appears as YHWH. This name of God was deemed too holy to be spoken by the Jews, so no vowels were added lest it be dishonored, even accidentally.

We have added consonants and have come to pronounce (or some would say mispronounce) the name as Jehovah. It means The Self-Existent One. No one brought Him into being. He owes His existence to no one but Himself.

We first see this name in Genesis 2:4 when we see God referenced as the One who created heaven and earth. It also means I Am, and I'll circle back to that in just a bit. And it also means Master, an appropriate name for the God who created our earth and everything in it.

Adonai

You will see it throughout the Old Testament, especially in the books of Isaiah, Ezekiel, and Daniel. It also means my great

Lord. This name speaks to how our relationship with God should look and we'll discuss that more later.

Yahweh Nissi

This means The Lord My Banner, My Miracle, My Refuge.

Moses, recognizing that the Lord was the banner under which the new nation of Israel defeated their enemies, the Amalekites, built an altar named JHWH Nissi (the Lord our Banner). Nes is sometimes translated as a pole with an insignia attached. In ancient times opposing nations would fly their flags on a pole at their respective front lines during battle. This was to give their soldiers a feeling of hope and a focal point. For a young nation struggling against opposing pagan peoples, you can probably see why this was an appropriate name for the God who was watching over them, protecting them from destruction.

Yahweh Yireh

Or Jehovah-Jireh, this name means The Lord Will Provide. We see this name used in Genesis 22, when Abraham (formerly known as Abram) goes to offer his son Isaac, the long-awaited baby he and his wife finally had, the child of promise, the greatest treasure of his heart, to God as a sacrifice. God intervened and instead provided a different sacrifice ... a ram caught in the thicket.

This can be such a difficult passage for many of us who are followers of Jesus. It certainly is for me. But I can understand the underlying message: God knows our needs. He will provide. This is also one of the names David uses for God in the 23rd Psalm (along with Yahweh-Rohi, which means shepherd).

Yahweh Rophe

This means The Lord Who Heals. Exodus 15:26 records God assuring the nation of Israel when they came out of slavery that as long as they trusted Him, He would keep them safe from the diseases common in the land of Egypt, home of their former masters, that He would be their healer.

This promise was made after three days in the desert without water. When they finally found some at a place called Marah (we're going to hear more about that name later), they couldn't drink it because it was bitter, so there was much complaining. I have to admit, I'd have probably been one of the loudest complainers!

God had no trouble fixing the problem. Exodus 15:25 shows us that the Lord of heaven and earth had a simple cure for the bitter waters. He showed Moses the wood from a certain tree with curative powers. Once Moses threw the wood into them it that took them from bitter to sweet.

Surely, we can count on that same God to turn the bitter waters of our own lives sweet.

Jehovah Shammah

The translation for this is the LORD is There; the LORD is My Companion. This name is used to describe the restored city of Jerusalem in Ezekiel's vision in Ezekiel 48:35 (the LORD is There). This same name is also used in Psalm 46. We start with the Old Testament, seeing His presence among His people, the nation of Israel.

We definitely see that the LORD is there in a story you may remember from Sunday School, the story of Shadrach, Meschach and Abednego. These ancient followers of God refused to cave and worship the god of the country in which their people were captives. In the third chapter of the book of Daniel in the Bible we read that the ruler, King Nebuchadnezzar, didn't take kindly to this civil disobedience, especially from men who had been granted important positions in the city of Babylon. The king was furious and ordered them put into a furnace heated seven times hotter than normal. His parting words to them were, "Then what god will be able to rescue you from my hand?"[3]

Theoretically, a story like that shouldn't have a happy ending. Unless you factor in God. It turns out our heroes weren't in that furnace alone. Another man was seen walking about with them,[4] a man who was nowhere to be found when they emerged safe and unharmed, not even smelling like smoke.[5] Not only did God protect them, not only was He with them in the fire, He showed his greatness to a pagan king.

These are a few of the many names given to God as recorded in Scripture. But I want to circle back to one that sums up all of these others.

I Am

YHWH, Yahweh, Jehovah – This says it all. And this is not a name given to God by man. This is the name God gives Himself. We can read about it in Exodus 3 when Moses, who led the Israelites out of Egyptian captivity, had his first conversation with the Almighty One.

It all started with Moses's curiosity over a burning bush in the desert where he lived. I'm sure, like me, you've read that in such a climate a burning bush in and of itself wasn't a unique phenomenon, that this had been known to happen thanks to spontaneous combustion. But for a bush to continue to burn without being consumed, now that was something worth investigating. So he drew closer.

That was when the angel of the LORD called his name. I must say, if my name was called from the midst of a fire anywhere, I'd have run like crazy. Moses, however, stayed and answered with, "Here I am."

It was the beginning of one of the most important conversations in history, with God assigning Moses the task of getting His enslaved people out of Egypt. All Moses had to do was go before Pharaoh and ask him to let an entire nation of slaves go. No problem.

Moses fretted, "Who am I that I should go to Pharaoh and bring the Israelites out of Egypt?"

God said, "I will be with you." (*Don't worry, Moses. I've got your back.*)

But Moses was still worried. He wanted to know what this conversation was going to look like. How was it going to turn out? In verse 13 of Exodus 3 we see him asking, "Suppose I go to the Israelites and say to them, 'The God of your fathers has sent me to you,' and they ask me, 'What is his name?' Then what shall I tell them?"

God answered quite succinctly. We see His reply in verse 14: "I AM WHO I AM. This is what you are to say to the Israelites: I AM has sent me to you."[6]

By the way, if you see LORD when reading the Old Testament, think Yahweh (the Existing One), that Being so great that we find ourselves returning to the all-encompassing label of Existing One, I Am.

I Am was enough for Moses. I Am is enough for us as well.

And what of His Son, Jesus Christ? Let's take a moment and look at His names. As with His (and our) heavenly Father, they are many. You can find them first listed in Isaiah 9:6: "For unto us a Child is born, unto us a Son is given; And the government will be upon His shoulder. And His name will be called Wonderful, Counselor, Mighty God, Everlasting Father, Prince of Peace."[7]

There are more names in addition to those.

Immanuel (Emmanuel)

Matthew 1:22, 23 quotes Isaiah 7:14 ("...The virgin will be with child and will give birth to a son and will call him Immanuel – which means 'God with us.'"[8]). Like His Father, Jesus was present among His people, living with them, teaching them, healing them, then, ultimately, sacrificing himself for them and for all who would come after them and believe in Him.

Jesus (Yeshua)

Actually, Yeshua is the shortened version of the name Yeshosuha or Joshua, which is the Hebrew word for Salvation. This was the perfect name, the name God specifically picked out for his Son because Jesus came to save God's people from their sins.[9]

We are clearly told in the Bible that there is no other name that packs the power of His, no other name will save us from our sin and ultimate judgement.[10] Jesus alone claims that honor and responsibility. Jesus alone rose from the dead and has the power to give life. "Therefore, God has highly exalted him and bestowed on him the name that is above every name, so that at the name of Jesus every knee should bow, in heaven and earth and under the earth, and every tongue confess that Jesus Christ is Lord..."[11]

Who Jesus is and what He's done qualify him to be so highly exalted. He is the Son of God, the essence of the Almighty Being who was poured into human flesh and willing to suffer and die for humanity. No other name ever has or ever will match up to his. No other name packs so much power or deserves such reverence.

Right now most of our world doesn't see that. This holy name is thrown around as a curse word, something to say in anger. But there will come a day when everyone will know who Jesus is and acknowledge Him as King of kings.

The Second Adam

In I Corinthians 15:45 Paul named Jesus The Second Adam. The first Adam, good old Earth Creature Adam, made of the dust of the earth, was the beginning of the human race, the beginning of physical life for us all. But his wrong choice brought death. Jesus, the Second Adam inhabited an earthly body, also, but was from heaven. Where the first Adam brought death, Jesus conquered it and brought spiritual rebirth and eternal life.

Truly the most impressive name of all is the one Jesus gave himself. You can find it in John 8:58.

I Am

There it is again!

In this chapter of John's account of the Lord's life here on earth we see Jesus having a discussion with His people, who were not liking what he was saying at all. He promised them they would never see death if they believed in Him, and their response was that He was demon possessed.[12]

As with many a good argument back then, the ancestors got brought into play. In this case Abraham (formerly known as Abram). And when Jesus said that Abraham rejoiced at the thought of seeing Jesus' arrival, his detractors sneered, "You are not yet fifty years old ... and you have seen Abraham?"[13]

Now came the amazing answer, the name that said exactly who Jesus was and is: "I tell you the truth," Jesus answered, "before Abraham was born, I am!"[14]

We've already seen the significance of that name. It's the very name the omnipotent, mighty God gave Himself. It's the same name that Moses heard coming out of that burning bush. Everyone knew the story. Everyone knew exactly what I Am meant.

I can only imagine how shocking this must have sounded coming from the lips of someone who appeared to be a mere man like everyone else. To the Jews, this statement was blasphemy, and they were ready to stone Jesus for saying such a thing.

Even Jesus' own disciples couldn't wrap their minds

around who He was. Things didn't start to clarify until after the resurrection.

It's still hard for us, with our finite minds, to comprehend the concept of God in the flesh, of what appeared to be a man turning out to be the Savior of the world, the Lamb of God who took away the sins of the world.[15] But comprehend it or not, it's true. Jesus' death finally paid the price for cosmic rebellion. The scales were set right. The sacrifice of His life brought an end to the need for the symbolic ritual of animal sacrifice because He was the ultimate, perfect sacrifice. Jesus bridged the gap and ended the self-inflicted estrangement between us and our Creator. Jesus was exactly who He said He was: the essence of truth and life, and the way to our heavenly Father.[16] He said, "Whoever has seen me has seen the Father."[17] He couldn't have been more clear about His identity than that.

Philippians 2:9-11 tells us that no name can compare to the name of Jesus. That is because of who He is. His name represents salvation and power. God exalted Him to the highest place – no Bible hero, no person in history can touch him in importance, none will receive the honor He will. Predicting that every knee in heaven and on earth and under the earth will bow covers it all.

Word of God

We see this in Revelation 19:13-15, where Jesus is depicted in a robe dipped in blood with the armies of heaven following him. We also see it in John 1:1 where the disciple John shortens the name to the Word. Do we want to know what God has to say to us? We will find it in the teachings of Jesus.

King of Kings, Lord of Lords

Here it is, in Revelation, right after we see our Lord depicted leading the armies of heaven: "On his robe and on his thigh he has his name written: KING OF KINGS AND LORD OF LORDS."[18] This is the same Lord who humbled himself and died a criminal's death on a cross. An ignoble end on earth, but in eternity our Lord reigns.

With our Almighty God in heaven, His Son seated at the right hand of his throne, that leaves us with one more important personage, the silent, mighty force that moves in our hearts and lives, the Spirit of God.

Holy Spirit

As much a mystery to us as God the Father and the Son, the Holy Spirit is given many titles: Counselor, Comforter, Advocate. We first see the Holy Spirit mentioned in Genesis 1:2, hovering over the waters of a formless, empty planet awaiting the creative hand of God, and we see Jesus promising to send this same Spirit to His disciples in John 14: 26.

The Holy Spirit is our helper, and our comfort. Romans 8:26-27 tells us that the Holy Spirit is also our intercessor. I Corinthians tells us that we are made clean and right with God by the power of the Holy Spirit. John 16:8 makes it clear that the Holy Spirit convicts us of guilt and shows us our need for a Savior. According to Galatians 5:23 the Holy Spirit gifts us with attributes our fallen selves don't come by naturally: love joy, peace, patience, kindness, goodness faithfulness, gentleness, and self-control. It is the Holy Spirit that enables us to grow spiritually.

Three in One

All these names for the amazing God we worship! One Being, three different facets. So, how can we apply these names to our daily lives? Please read on.

1. I used many sources researching God's names. *The Names of God*, published by Hendrickson Rose Publishing, May 2018, 9th printing. Also, I

researched on many online sites, including the following:

THE BLUE LETTER BIBLE.ORG, https://www. blueletterbible.org/study/misc/name_god.cfm; Bible Study Tools, https://www.biblestudytools.com/bible-study/topical-studies/why-it-matters-that-god-is-yahweh.html; Bibleinfo.com, https://www.bibleinfo.com/en/questions/names-of-god, Truth or Tradition.com, https://www.truthortradition.com/articles/yhwh-the-name-of-god, ChristianAnswers.net, https://christiananswers.net/dictionary/namesofgod.html

1. Genesis 16:13
2. New International Version
3. Daniel 3:15, New International Version
4. Daniel 3:25
5. Daniel 3:26, 27
6. New International Version
7. New King James Version
8. New International Version
9. Matthew 1:21
10. Acts 4:12
11. Philippians 2:9, 10, English Standard Version
12. John 8:48
13. John 8:57, New International Version
14. John 8:58, New International Version
15. John 1:29
16. John 14:6
17. John 14:9, English Standard Version
18. Revelation 19:16, English Standard Version

THREE
WHAT'S IT TO ME? PRACTICAL APPLICATION

As we've seen, the names for God carry with them definitions of his character. They define who He is, what He's done, and what He's capable of doing. Let's break this down a little and see how the truth of these names applies to our lives.

El Elyon, the Most High

It's easy to look at everything happening in our world and feel worried or insecure because events outside our control can impact our lives in negative ways. We see violence and cruelty around us, nature hits us with hurricanes, tornadoes, tropical storms, and pandemics. Fires break out. It's a dangerous world out there.

But our God, El Elyon, is the Most High. He outranks and is more powerful than the highest power in both this world and the unseen one. Nothing touches us without His permission. Romans 8:31 says it all: "... If God is for us who can be against us?"[1] If we can remember that we can have peace, no matter what's going on around us.

El Shaddai, the Nurturing Strong One

Our God is not only mighty, but He is also a caring God.

He didn't simply create our planet, set it spinning, and then ignore it. He populated it with living creatures. He lovingly and creatively formed humankind out of the dust of the earth. And when those first humans failed to obey Him, He balanced punishment with love and clothed them.[2] He provided food for an escaping slave nation.[3] He sacrificed His own Son.[4]

He hasn't changed. He still cares for His people. We can bring our concerns and our problems to Him and know that He will work in us, through us and for us. During those times you are tempted to doubt this read I Peter 5:7. That verse gives us permission to throw off our worries onto God. We don't need to carry them.

El Roi, the God Who Sees

Ever ask, "God, don't you see what I'm going through?" The answer to that would be, "Yes, He does." Jesus said the Father knows and holds in His hands even the life of the small sparrow that falls to the ground.[5] Think of Job (who still holds the record for the man who's suffered the most). The book of the Bible named after him tells of his loss of family, all his possessions and then his health. Job was one miserable mortal. And yet God saw what He was going through. It was God who reminded Job that He is God and that His ways aren't our ways. And it was God who, when Job's sufferings were over, blessed him. God saw, God knew, God didn't desert. God won't desert us in our dark times, either. That doesn't mean we won't have them living in this imperfect world, but it does mean we will get through them.

No matter what you're going through, whether it's a mess you stepped into by taking a wrong turn, an unexpected event that crashed on you like a storm or something someone has done to you, God is aware of it. You can know that and rest in it even if you don't understand the why of it.

El Olam, our Eternal God

I think this is one of the most wonderful and comforting characteristics of our God. People come and go from our lives. Friends move away and move on. Parents die. So do spouses. Divorce happens. We cannot count on our fellow human beings to always be around. But we can count on God. Because He is everlasting, He will be with us through this life and the one to come.

Adonai, Our Master

Master means exactly that. What the master says is law. The master decides the fate of his servants. The master is in control and the servants know it. This is a scary proposition if the master is human. But our Master is not. Our Master is gracious, patient, and loving. However, He still is Lord.

I admit that I use the term Lord a lot – Thank you, Lord ... Help me, Lord ... Are you listening, Lord? – but I often forget what that really means. It means that I answer to a higher power. I have a Master to serve, a Master to whom I owe my life, in both this world and the next. It's not all about Him serving my wants and needs. (Although He does meet my needs. And more!) It's about doing things with my time, my money, my mouth that serve Jesus, God's Son. He is Lord of lords and King of kings, and I am in His service. I don't get to re-invent or circumvent His word.

That's actually a good thing because His word is true, and His laws are just. The rules our God lays down are meant to keep us safe and well, both individually and as a society. We can trust that He who made us has our best interests at heart. Serving Him gives us a purpose and gives our lives meaning. When we honor him, we honor others as well because His love commands us to. When our God is truly our Lord everybody benefits. Imagine how empty and fruitless your life would be without God!

Yahweh Nissi, my Banner, my Refuge

Who can I turn to in times of trouble? Not the government, not always. Governments try, but people fall through the cracks. Governments even collapse, leaving people in chaos. And, looking at history, we can see that some governments, such as Hitler's Nazi regime, not only fail to protect people but abuse them terribly.

If not the government, how about my savings? Surely there is security in that nest egg.

Unless your retirement account is depending on the stock market and that takes a dive. Unless inflation hits. Nest eggs only last so long, especially during a depression or recession. Even real estate, which is traditionally thought to be a sound investment, can turn out to be not so sound.

Well, then, my spouse. Sure, as long as you don't divorce, or your other half doesn't die.

The kids. The kids will take care of me in my old age. But what if you outlive your children? Then what?

There is only One whom we can ultimately trust, who can provide wisdom, comfort, and emotional shelter in hard times and that is God.

The third and fourth verses of Psalm 91 give us a lovely image. Here they are in the New King James Bible translation: "He shall cover you with His feathers and under His wings you shall take refuge." I love the visual of this. Can't you just picture a mother hen, gathering her chicks under her to protect them? Can you now envision yourself standing under the shadow of the mighty God?

In Psalm 4:8 the psalmist determines to lie down and sleep in peace because he knows that God allows him to dwell in safety. We can sleep at night because we can take refuge under the protection of our mighty God.

I've heard people say, "The universe was watching over me," or, "The universe is trying to tell me something." The universe doesn't care that we exist. It is simply there. But the One who created the universe – that's a different story. He is watching over us. And, unlike the universe, He actually does care what happens to us. There is no place in the universe where we can shelter, but we can find shelter and hope in our God.

When you feel like the foundations of your world are shaking, Psalm 20:7 is a good verse to memorize: "Some trust in chariots and some in horses but we trust in the name of the LORD our God."[6] – the name of the One who is our banner, our shelter. Since this was written at a time when armies looked very different than they do today, feel free to substitute other more modern nouns for chariots and horses. Perhaps bank accounts. Or Congress or the military. Not that we don't want to have money in savings or that we don't appreciate getting a tax refund or living in times of peace. But the foundation under all that is the Lord. Things may get shaky, but that foundation never fails.

We all have spiritual battles to fight, temptations that are hard to resist. Some of us might have fought (and could still be fighting) a serious addiction or struggling with food issues. Some of us may struggle to be patient and understanding. Some of us struggle with poor self-image while still others of us find it difficult to let go of grudges. Any time we decide to lose harmful attitudes and behaviors and make positive changes in our lives it's a battle. And if we are trying to accomplish something noble, we can know for sure that we will have a fight on our hands. The higher the calling, the more that is at stake, the greater the battle.

But we fight under the banner of the Most High God. He is our miracle; He gives us strength. He is our refuge when the battle gets heated and when we experience battle fatigue, He will give us strength. Romans 8:37 tells us that in everything we can be more than conquerors. We not only have the ability to win those spiritual battles, but we can also drive the enemy into the ground.

Whatever you may be fighting, know that you don't have to face it alone. Prayer and Scripture will be your weapons and you can win because of Who is on your side.

Yahweh (Jehovah) Jireh, the LORD Will Provide for Me

How many times in the Bible have we seen God do this for His people? Think of Noah in the ark, sheltering during the great flood.[7] Or the young nation of Israel surviving on the mysterious Manna. Let's also remember the Old Testament account of the widow in Israel who made one small meal for the prophet Elijah during a time of famine, and in turn wound up with enough oil and flour to live on until the rains came and crops could grow once more.[8] Let's think about Jesus, pointing Simon Peter the fisherman to the fish that would give him the money to pay his taxes.[9]

Stories of God's provision aren't confined to the Bible. Have you ever read *The Hiding Place*, the memoir of Corrie ten Boom, the Dutch woman who sheltered so many Jews from the Nazis in World War II? She and her sister wound up in Ravensbrück concentration camp. She wrote of how horrible the fleas were in their women's barracks. Great cruelty was being heaped on these women, but God provided refuge, using something as small as a flea to turn that barracks into a place of shelter from the abuse of the guards. The guards refused to enter because of the fleas.

Yes, thanks to the cruelty of the soldiers and the corrupt government, women died in that camp. (As with the sparrow Jesus mentioned, God was aware of it and ready to take them in His arms, putting an end to their suffering forever.) But women survived as well, including Corrie, who went on to live an amazing life.

When we're in that dark cave of trouble we can't always see ahead to the light beyond it, but God does. We may not know where the money's going to come from to pay the bills or put food on the table. We may not know where we're going to find that much needed job, that place to live, that godly mate, but God knows.

I love King David's observation in Psalm 37:25: "I have been young, and no am old; yet I have not seen the righteous forsaken, nor his descendants begging bread."

I can certainly testify to seeing the truth of that in my own life. My husband and I have gone through hard times where money was tight, but God always provided for us. Sometimes this involved being able to pick up an extra job, sometimes it was a box of groceries left anonymously on our porch. There were some times when plain old scrounging and gleaning were involved, but we never went hungry.

Can you think of a time when God brought someone into your life to help you fix your car? Or loan you some money? Provide a bag of groceries when your cupboard was just about empty? How about a much-needed job? The Lord will provide.

Yahweh Rophe, Our God Who Heals

James 5:14 tells us to call our church leaders to come pray for us when we're sick. My husband and I did this when I was diagnosed with uterine cancer. I will always be grateful to the men who took time to do this for us. I was surprised and saddened when one of them remarked how rarely people in the church asked their elders to pray for their healing. Are you dealing with illness right now? Make the call!

God might use you to pray for someone who is sick. I'm grateful for my friend Hilda, one of the members of my church, whose ministry is to pray with people for healing when they're sick. Hilda's great faith and powerful prayers have released the power of God our healer in my life on more than one occasion.

And she, herself, bears testimony to the power of God after receiving healing when cancer returned to her body a second time and tried to take her down. It was a miraculous healing that spared her from having to undergo chemotherapy.

God has equipped our bodies with an immune system that works to fight off illness and keep us in good repair. Broken bones re-knit, cuts heal. We come down with a cold and our body instantly goes into battle mode. And don't forget nerves. Think of the service your nerves do you. You touch something hot, and they scream, "Get your hand away from that!" thus preventing further damage. All this by design, all this thanks to the God who heals us.

Let's not lose sight of other provisions that we tend to think of as separate from God. Doctors, medicines, vaccines, nutritious food, healing plants such as Aloe Vera – how many wonderful tools God has provided for our well-being!

It's not always our bodies that need healing. The most vital healing any of us need is that of our hearts and minds. Even more important than the wellness of the body is the wellness of the soul, and our God has provided for that. Isaiah 53:5 tells us that Jesus suffered so we could be made well. "He was beaten so we could be whole, He was whipped so we could be healed."[11]

Jehovah Shammah, the LORD is There for You

The Lord is there? Where? Wherever His people are. The God who created us does not abandon us. He has always been there, even in the darkest of times, when have been inexcusably, damnably cruel to each other. No matter what troubles come to us, no matter what the powers of darkness throw at us, we never face them alone.

Immanuel (Emmanuel), Our God is with Us

Jesus became the visible manifestation of the invisible Jehovah Shammah so long followed by so many. His miracles and his resurrection proved who he was. He changed lives and the people whose lives he changed went on to change the world.

But they didn't do it alone. Jesus promised His disciples He would never leave or forsake them. After His resurrection, He sent His Holy Spirit, not only to them but to those who heard the good news of His resurrection and committed themselves to following Him.[12.] He still sends His Holy Spirit to all who believe in Him.

So our God has always and is always there, first as Jehovah Shammah of the Old Testament, then as Jesus, our Emmanuel of the New Testament. Today His Holy Spirit is still with us. We are not and never will be alone.

This means that we always have someone to tell our troubles to, someone who won't get tired of listening, who will be with us through the storms of life, just as He was in the boat with His disciples on that stormy day on the sea of Galilee. Mark 4: 35-41 tells us that all was well when Jesus and the disciples got into a boat to cross to the other side. Until a squall came up, changing everything.

Isn't that how life often goes? One minute all is fine. The next minute we find ourselves in a typhoon. But Jesus was there in the boat with His disciples and He's with us as well when we are scared. There's no need for fear. He calmed the storm for the disciples, and He can calm the storm in us if we keep our eyes on Him, not on the lightning and the high waves.

I first started working on this book during a time when there was a lot of fear all over the world. COVID-19 had come along and turned our lives upside down, either with illness and death and financial trouble or with a complete disruption of our daily routines. People are panicked.

I was certainly tempted to be. Early on, when the pandemic was first spreading, I caught some kind of a bug and was on antibiotics. It lingered long after the antibiotics, and I'll confess I had a couple of sleepless nights when I kept swallowing, testing to see if my throat was getting sore, which was what I'd heard was the first symptom of trouble. Was I coming down with the COVID-19 virus?

Then I read Jesus' words to His disciples after he'd calmed the wind. We read in Mark 4:40, "Why are you so afraid? Do you still have no faith?"[13.] I thought of all the things the Lord has brought me through, from cancer to a faulty heart that needed fixing, to name a few, and I asked myself, "Why, indeed?" God knows the number of my days. My life is in His hands, so there's no need to worry. This might be something you need to tell yourself as well.

No matter what storm may be raging, we are not in it alone. Immanuel is with us. We can rest in that knowledge.

Are you going through something difficult right now? Let me share this piece of timeless advice from Philippians 4: 5-8: "...The Lord is near. Do not worry about anything, but in everything by prayer and supplication with thanksgiving let your requests be made known to God. And the peace of God, which surpasses all understanding, will guard your hearts and your minds in Christ Jesus."[14.]

Remember that the Lord is near. Don't allow yourself to fret and stew. It's a waste of time. Instead, tell God what you need. Remember to be thankful for His presence.

What are we told will happen when we do this? Our God, who is with us, will give us peace.

Here's another important Scripture to remember: "For where two or three are gathered in my name I am there among them."[15.] Just as He was with His disciples, our Lord is with us, His followers. Praying together reminds us that we are all part of something bigger than ourselves. The Lord hears. His Spirit is right there, listening.

Having friends or family sharing our concerns and also praying encourages us, and it is important to gather together. But whether we're physically with other believers or isolated, no matter what, Jesus, our Immanuel, is always with us thanks to His Holy Spirit.

Jesus Our Salvation

Mary and Joseph didn't have to throw ideas back and forth for baby names for her firstborn son. It had already been picked out for them by God, Himself. In Matthew 1:20, 21 we read, "... an angel of the LORD appeared to him in a dream and said, 'Joseph, son of David, do not be afraid to take Mary home as your wife because what is conceived in her is from the Holy Spirit. She will give birth to a son, and you are to give him the name Jesus because He will save His people from their sins.'"[16.]

Remember, the name Jesus a form of Joshua, which is the word for salvation. You might remember another Joshua, one from the Old Testament who followed Moses as leader of the nation of Israel and took them into the Promised Land. Joshua was a great leader, but his role was a physical one, taking a people into a physical land. Jesus came to do something immeasurably more important – He came to take His people into Paradise, to save them from their sinful condition, reunite them with their Creator and give them a new life. Jesus really is the Name above all names, and we can look to Him to deliver us from the eternal consequences of sin.

His name carries with it the authority of the Father. Remember, Jesus said He and the Father are one. To his disciples, so anxious to see God, Himself, Jesus said, "He who has seen Me has seen the Father..."[17.] In other words... well, there are no other words. Jesus was God in the flesh, the human representation of something human eyes would not otherwise get to see. He is the Prince of Peace, Son of the most high God.

What does that mean for us? For one, it means that we can pray in His name and expect answers.

In John 14:13 He promised His disciples that He would do whatever they asked in His name. It was like having the royal seal. It gave them spiritual power here on earth. But this wasn't a power that was to be misused. It was power with a purpose. Jesus went on to explain to them that this was so that God, His father, would be glorified.

And He was. Using that power, Jesus' disciples healed the lame,[18.] Raised people from the dead,[19.] And shook off poisonous snakes[20.] (Acts 28:3-6). Jesus' people prayed for their leader, Peter, to be freed from prison and an angel gave him a personal escort to freedom.[21.]

We, his followers, have access to that same power. We, too, carry the royal seal on our hearts. When we are walking close to God, we can have confidence our prayers will be answered.

Having said that, I know that often we ask for, beg for certain things and don't see our prayers answered in a way we would like. I have no pat answer for that, other than sometimes we are not asking for the right thing. Sometimes God has a bigger plan than our small ones. Sometimes we ask things not knowing the ramifications of our request.

I think of King Hezekiah in the Bible. He was a righteous man and a good king. He had a good life, and he was in no hurry to leave it. But then came the day when God's prophet came to him and said, "This is it. Get your house in order. It's time for you to die." Hezekiah went into pout mode. The Bible account tells us he turned his face to the wall, wept bitterly, and begged for more time.[22.] God answered that prayer, allowing him another fifteen years, but as a result of his longer life span a lot of things played out in the nation that could have been avoided if he'd accepted God's decree.

For one, he lived to entertain ambassadors from Babylon.

These men were the ancient equivalent of a get-well card, and, happy to have visitors, Hezekiah gave them a tour of his treasure house – all the silver and gold and precious ointments, and the armory.[23.] I bet you can guess the end results of this. Further down the road Babylon invaded, carrying away all the treasures and taking the people as slaves.[22.]

Hezekiah's son, Manasseh, was born during those extra fifteen years. (Oh, boy, a son!) Except Manasseh did not grow up to be a credit to his father. He was one of the most wicked kings in Israel's history and would become the land of Judah's downfall.[25.]

Hezekiah couldn't see ahead to all of this. He only knew what he wanted.

As do we all. But none of us can see the future.

Our firstborn child, a daughter, was severely handicapped. She never learned to crawl or walk or talk in spite of the fact that, when she was a baby, we prayed for her healing. Our entire church fasted and prayed for it. I expected it, I was sure God had given me a Bible verse as a promise that she would be healed. It didn't happen and I eventually came to realize that Bible verse was meant to be a comfort for us rather than a prediction of a change in our daughter's condition.

Years later I was complaining to God about this, asking why He didn't answer my prayers. The answer I received was, "I did. Now, stop asking." This wasn't said meanly, but like a parent explaining reality to a child who just didn't get it.

I wondered what prayer I could possibly have prayed that would have resulted in this. And then I remembered. I was a newlywed, living in Germany with my husband. I can still see myself in the little church where we worshiped, kneeling at a pew and praying, "God, I've had such a good life, with no real trials or troubles. Please give me trials so I can be a witness and an encouragement to others."

What was I thinking! I honestly don't know. One thing I know, I hadn't wanted a trial to look like this.

You may be thinking to yourself, *Yeah, right. God spoke to her.* Or, *As if God would be so cruel.* Let me just say that God was not cruel, but as with all of us living in a fallen world, He allowed me to experience some of a small amount of the human suffering we see all around us.

We lost our daughter a few years ago. The night after she died, I saw her in my dreams – healed and happy. Finally, just as with that long ago prayer, my prayers for her healing were answered. Certainly not the way I'd expected but I can live with that because I know I will see her again in a perfect, new body.

So, why am I sharing these two very different life stories, one of a king, an important Biblical figure, and one of woman of no historical significance? Simply to say that our prayers have power because we pray in the name of the Lord to our Almighty Father. Our prayers set off things in a realm we cannot see. Because they have such power, it's important that our first and foremost prayer every day be, "God, give me Your wisdom," and every request should end with "Not my will but Yours be done." Because God sees far out into eternity and God, the true and perfect father, knows what's best.

We need God's wisdom because sometimes our prayers can be simply selfish and wrong, and if we're not asking for His wisdom, we may not see it. In James 3:4 believers were told that they sometimes didn't get what they asked for because their prayers were selfish, and they were thinking primarily of their pleasure. Without God's wisdom it's easy to turn a blind eye to underlying motives behind our prayers. Do we ask God to provide transportation so we can get to work, or do we pray for the money to buy that cool convertible the neighbor is selling? Do we ask for a house and picture a mansion? How pure and selfless are our requests? If they're not so pure, if to have those requests answered will harm us spiritually, they might not be answered the way we want.

Our Lord isn't a genie, waiting to grant our every wish. Let's keep that in mind when we are invoking His name and consider carefully what we ask for in that name. I believe we should bow to God's authority when we get answers to our prayers, no matter what the answers are because He does see the big picture that we can't see.

Let's remember that God is a good God, not willing that any of us should be lost to Him.[26.] To that end, He works through our prayers and in our lives, to show His glory and, often to bring others to Himself. When you pray in the name of Jesus, know that you pray with power, and you can expect an answer. You can also know that God will work to accomplish His perfect will (which may not always line up with what you asked for).

I am convinced it was the prayers of God's people that healed me of cancer, that He healed me for His purposes, not mine. (Although I admit that sometimes I lose track of that important fact.) I am convinced that He cares for you, and wants you to put forward your requests with thanksgiving, invoking His name. The same promise He gave His disciples holds true for His followers today.

YHWH, Yahweh, Jehovah, I Am

Here is the ultimate answer to all our questions? We ask, "Who is my provider?" God says, "I Am." We ask, "Who is the one I can turn to in times of trouble?" God says, "I Am." We ask, "Who knows the number of my days? Who is the one who ultimately decides when I leave this earth and when I stay?" God answers, "I Am."

Who can we trust? Where can we shelter in times of need? Who cares the most for us? The answer is always God,

Yahweh, Jehovah, the mighty I Am. Who cared enough to heal our broken lives, to clean up the mess we made of ourselves and restore our sin-stained souls, to give us hope by sending us a Savior? Yes, it is God. We can take great comfort in this knowledge.

When we face challenges and hard times, when we're unsure about important decisions, when we're struggling with relationship problems, when questions arise – the answer can always be found in God. We can still our troubled minds and worried hearts by applying those names of God and all they represent to our circumstances.

When we feel alone in our struggle and ask ourselves, "Does anyone see? Does anyone care?" The answer is yes, El Roi sees and cares. When we're worried about job security, our retirement fund, our children's college education, when we ask, "Where's the money going to come from?" the answer is Yahweh Jireh, the LORD will provide. He owns the world and all that is in it – the cattle on a thousand hills, every bird and creature.[27.] Meeting our needs is no challenge for Him.

When we fall sick, we can call out to Yahweh Rophe, the God Who Heals. He not only heals our hurts and spiritual wounds, He even takes away the sting of death![28.]

When we are afraid and all seems lost and we cry out, "Where can I turn?" the answer is to turn to the great I Am. He is our refuge.

Are you dealing with some kind of addiction, trying to lose weight, battling to control your temper? Perhaps you're struggling with a difficult co-worker, or you have a child with physical challenges or a learning disability. You may find yourself asking, "Who's going to help me with this?" God answers, "I Am." He cares enough to save us, give us wisdom and help us win our battles. Whatever we face, whatever the powers of darkness throw in our path, we are not alone. God, the great I Am, is with us.

King David sums up our relationship with our God beautifully in the 23rd Psalm:

> The LORD is my shepherd; I shall not want
> He makes me lie down in green pastures;
> He leads me beside still waters.
> He restores my soul;
> He leads me in the paths of righteousness for His name's sake
> Yea, though I walk through the valley of the Shadow of Death,
> I will fear no evil;
> For You are with me;
> Your rod and Your staff, they comfort me.
> You prepare a table for me in the presence of my enemies;
> You anoint my head with oil;
> My cup runs over.
> Surely goodness and mercy will follow me
> All the days of my life;
> And I will dwell in the house of the LORD forever.[29.]

We serve a mighty, multi-faceted, unfathomable, loving, all-powerful God. Keeping that in mind, we can live victorious, light-filled, meaningful lives.

1. New International Version
2. Genesis 3:21
3. Exodus 16:13-31
4. John 3:16
5. Matthew 10:29
6. New International Version
7. Genesis 7:23

8. I Kings 17: 1-16
9. Matthew 17:24-27
10. New King James Version
11. New Living Translation
12. Acts 2:1-4
13. New International Version
14. New Revised Standard Version
15. Matthew 18:20, New Revised Standard Version
16. New Revised Standard Version
17. John 14:9, New King James Version
18. Acts 3:1-11
19. Acts 9:36-43;
20. Acts 20:9-12
21. Acts 12: 1-11
22. 2 Kings 20:1-3
23. 2 Kings 20: 12-18
24. 2 Chronicles 33: 10,11
25. 2 Kings 21:1-16
26. 2 Peter 3:9
27. Psalm 50:10-12
28. 1 Corinthians 15:54-56
29. New International Version

FOUR
HELLO, MY NAME IS ...

What we call ourselves needs to line up with who our God is. As His children our names are inextricably linked with His and that should color the way we see ourselves.

But we live in a fallen world filled with challenges and distractions, and it's easy to forget that we are children of the great I Am. When we lose our focus on Him and His purpose for our lives, when we fail to apply all that, His name means in every situation and every time we look in the mirror, we start seeing ourselves through a false filter.

Using that false filter, we give ourselves names that shine darkness on us rather than light, that taint the way we see ourselves and our life. Tainted vision can't help but produce discouragement, fear, bitterness.

A good example of this is Naomi, one of my favorite women of the Bible. She's an interesting woman and a true heroine. We find her story in the book of Ruth.

Let's take a look at her life. It started with a measure of practicality. Famine hit the land of Judah and Ruth's husband moved her and their two boys to the country of Moab, hoping for a better life.

Sadly, that didn't happen. Her husband died. She and her sons stayed on in Moab and the boys wound up marrying a couple of the local girls. Then tragedy struck again and both Ruth's sons died. We're not told how they died. We only know she lost them, and with them she lost everything. It was time to go home.

One daughter-in-law kissed her good-bye and stayed behind. The other, Ruth, committed to going back to Judah with Naomi.

Here's where our story gets interesting.

When Naomi and Ruth arrived in Naomi's hometown of Bethlehem her friends and neighbors were excited to see her and could scarcely believe their eyes. "Naomi, is it really you?"

Naomi answered: "... 'Do not call me Naomi; call me Mara, for the Almighty has dealt very bitterly with me. I went out full, and the LORD has brought me home again empty. Why do you call me Naomi, since the LORD has testified against me, and the Almighty has afflicted me?'"[3.]

The name Naomi means pleasantness. But Mara means bitter. (Remember the waters that the escaped slaved nation of Israel found undrinkable and what that place was called!) Naomi was no longer happy with the name she had, and she took it on herself to change the beautiful one she'd been given into something that symbolized where she was emotionally.

And she laid the blame squarely on God. It was all His fault that her husband had died, that she'd lost her sons. It was all God's fault that the family left the Promised Land and moved to a pagan land. Look what He'd done to her. How could he have allowed these things to happen?

Have you ever done that? Maybe not as blatantly as Naomi, but have you thought of yourself as unloved, cursed, unappreciated? Have you felt that God was dealing unfairly with you? Maybe right now you're reading this and saying, "Yes, that name fits me perfectly." Perhaps you've let your circumstances color the way you see yourself and your life. Maybe, like Naomi, you have given up.

Naomi was sure her story was over. She came home defeated, ready to live out the rest of her days in bitterness. But she had this young woman in tow, one who looked to her for guidance. She had someone besides herself to think about. Soon Naomi found herself acting as confidante and advisor to Ruth, who had found an admirer in a well-off man named Boaz.

Naomi began to take an interest in life once more – mainly the love life of her daughter-in-law. Like most of us women, she appreciated a good love story, and she was happy to help this one along, advising Ruth every step of the way.

Suddenly, things were looking up, and in Ruth 2:20, we see Naomi changing her tune about God and saying, "...He has not stopped showing his kindness to the living and the dead."[4.] What a different tune she was beginning to sing from the one she sang when she first hit town.

This is what we writers refer to as character development. Naomi's eyes began to open to the goodness of God. Yes, she had gone through horrible loss. She had suffered. But her life wasn't over. There was so much more to be lived. God had a plan and He allowed Naomi to be part of it. And she began to see that.

Her story had a happy ending. Ruth and Boaz married and had a son named Obed.

And Naomi, who had come home so heartbroken and bitter, found the rainbow after the storm. She went from having no husband or sons to care for her to having a son-in-law to watch out for her and a grandchild to help nurture. Her grandchild, Obed, became the father of Jesse, who became the father of King David of Israel. Naomi was not only blessed with family once more, but she was also allowed to play a very important role in a story that had a huge impact on her people. Her life started out small but, in the end, became part of something large.

I find it telling that the name she gave herself didn't stick. She is never referred to in the narrative of the book of Ruth as Mara. And in our happy ending scene, we hear her neighbors saying, "Praise be to the LORD, who this day has not left you without a kinsman-redeemer."[5.] In other words, "Look, God has provided for you."

God knew the end of Naomi's story, and it wasn't bitter. It was pleasant.

Perhaps, like Naomi, difficult circumstances have convinced you to give yourself a name that reflects your discouragement. But, as with Naomi, that name isn't the one God wants for you. Like Naomi, there might be much more to the picture than you are seeing. There may be people in your life right now who could use your friendship and support, perhaps your wisdom. You may have learned some hard lessons and maybe those lessons need to be shared with someone facing challenges similar to what you've faced.

Many of us let our circumstances motivate us to pick negative names to hang onto, names that turn our focus onto those circumstances rather than the One who will enable us to rise above them.

Often we let others determine our identity with the things they say and do to us, giving us an inaccurate picture of how God sees us. We buy the lie and tune our attitude and behavior to it. Or we spend time looking for inappropriate ways to disprove it.

How were you treated as a child? As a teenager? How have

you been treated as an adult? Were you called names? Was there a specific name that burrowed into your mind and reshaped how you saw yourself?

If so, you're not alone. I put out a call on my Facebook like page, inviting women to share their stories about how names they were called had affected them, both positively and negatively, and I had over a hundred comments in the first hour. Sadly, most of those comments shared negative experiences and name calling.

I think of June, who said she was chubby as a child. Other children nicknamed her June Balloon. Too embarrassed to publicly post her story in the conversational thread, she messaged me privately and shared about how that hurt affected her. She gave me her permission to tell her story here, and I appreciate her bravery in allowing me to do so.

"It still has an effect on how I see myself today," she wrote. "Weight has always been an issue. Self-esteem low."

Another woman who had weight issues as a young teen was nicknamed Dino after the dinosaur in the old cartoon show *The Flintstones*. "Being made fun of impacts your emotional state (you never forget) and I've had to develop a tough skin," she wrote. "It's contributed to depression periods and continued food gratification dependency." Clearly, a deep wound lies under that tough skin.

Another woman reported that as a young girl she was teased because of her height and bullied. "A horrible neighborhood duo graffitied 'goon girl' on the garage at our house and would yell it at me whenever they saw me. I became so introverted I didn't want to leave the house. I am so sad to think of that young girl now and what she missed because of the name calling," she finished.

One of my beautiful writing friends was called Buck Tooth in elementary and middle school. She says, "To this day I can't look at my teeth without pain." I look at her and see her gorgeous eyes and nose and lovely smile. I've never noticed her teeth!

Another woman shared that she didn't fit in at school. She was ostracized and called names like Freak and Retard.

One would like to think this sort of thing stops when we grow up, but, sadly, it doesn't. My good writing buddy Jill is both beautiful and talented, but even she had an unpleasant memory to share. "A rather vicious 'friend' started calling me Wilbur at work. It was for Wilber the pig in *Charlotte's Web*. I tried to laugh it off, put on a brave face, but it wasn't very kind. She got others to call me that like they were just teasing. It always hurt."

Yes, those words surely do. My friend Karen says, "I'd rather you hit me than say unkind things to me."

I think many of us would agree. Physical bruises heal. Emotional ones can fester.

I think of another lovely woman who confided her story to me. Childhood names followed her clear into adulthood and affected her relationships. She often found herself with men who would insult her and tell her how unworthy of love she was and that she should be glad they were deigning to be with her.

Like many of the women who told their stories to me, I was given a name in high school that rode around with me for half of my adult life. It was given me by my high school choir director.

I can still see myself, sitting in a chair in the choir room before class, visiting with a friend. Happy, flirting a little. In walked our choir director, a funny, high-energy man all of us kids loved.

I'm sure his greeting was meant to be flippant when he

smiled and said to my friend, "What are you doing talking to that ugly duckling?" But I wasn't able to take it lightly.

Ugly duckling. Okay, I knew I wasn't as cute as my cheerleader girlfriend, but ugly? People saw me as ugly.

Looking back, I wish I'd told my mother what this teacher had said. Maybe she'd have reminded me that in the famous Hans Christian Andersen story the ugly duckling grew into a beautiful swan.

I didn't tell her. I didn't tell anyone. Instead, I took this teacher's words to heart. I was not pretty. Who was ever going to want me?

In fairness to the teacher, I'm sure he had no idea what effect his comment had on me. He'd had my brothers in choir. He and my dad were both members of the local Lion's Club. Maybe he felt that gave him permission to tease me. Who knows?

All I know is that his words left me feeling inadequate. I spent a great deal of time over the next twenty years trying to prove to myself that I wasn't ugly. I was desirable.

The insecurity that had embedded itself in my brain stayed there, even after I found a wonderful man who loved me and thought I was beautiful. It grew like a tree, continuing to drop its poison leaves into my psyche. No matter how cute I tried to be, no matter how I dressed or how much makeup I applied, the poison tree whispered, "Ugly." I had to prove it wrong.

In my thirties I was coming close. I'd lost weight after our baby boy was born; a stylist friend gave me a makeover. I started singing in bands, all dolled up and wearing heels like Tina Turner. I was rocking the new me as hard as I could and getting a good share of male admiration. Maybe I wasn't so ugly after all.

Except admiration isn't always kept at a distance. Suddenly,

I had men in my life who would be happy to step in and make me happy if my husband couldn't. One of them promised to make me a star. I look back on that time and thank God that He kept me from doing anything stupid to wreck my marriage. He opened my eyes and reminded me what a wonderful husband I had. The band chick phase ended, and it was time to concentrate on raising children. The poison tree had been chopped down.

But not pulled up by the root. I still knew my real name: Ugly Duckling. Even though I had finally pulled myself together and was looking good, something new had reared its head. I was aging. Oh, no! Already? I'd barely gotten it together and now it was falling apart.

I look back and wonder what on earth I was thinking to be obsessed with wrinkles in my forties. (I think I had maybe two.) Oh, yes, I was thinking *Ugly Duckling*. Everyone knows you can't be pretty and old at the same time, right? Bad enough that I still hated my nose and my long face. Now I had to worry about wrinkles around my lips and drooping skin. Soon I'd have drooping... everything. I would be coming full circle, back to ugly. Only now I had a new name to tack on to Ugly Duckling: Old. As if being blessed with a long life is a bad thing!

This all seems so silly of me, doesn't it? But when we buy into negative names we don't see clearly. As I consider all the ads for Botox, liposuction and wrinkle cream, it's clear to me that there is a multitude of us who have bought into our culture's limited definition of beauty.

For the most part I've moved on. In fact, I look back at pictures of myself in my thirties and wonder why I thought I was so ugly. Good grief.

Still, a bit of that root lingers. It seems I'm always pulling up a fresh sprout. Sometimes I look in the mirror and, for a moment, I sigh, and wish I was young again.

Satan, of course, would love for me to look at myself and see all the flaws. He'd delight in getting me to feel like less and adopt those negative names. But I know that nothing good comes from playing that losing game.

So, what do I do when my mirror fails to tell me I'm the fairest of them all, when I remember that old moniker of Ugly Duckling, when I'm tempted to pine for the days of fresh, dewy, unwrinkled skin? When I bemoan my now white hair? I thank God that I'm still here. I could have died from uterine cancer in 2013 but it was detected in time and God has graciously allowed me more years with my family and friends. Is that worth the price of some wrinkles and white hair? I'd say so. Many people die young. They never live to see their children grow up, never get to see all their dreams come true. Long life is a privilege.

I also ask God to help me remember there is more to life than being beautiful. When I covet and strive for beauty, I'm turning it into an idol. My focal point should be God, not my mirror.

Beauty, like all gifts, comes from God, so I'm not going to begrudge any woman her because physical beauty reflects back to our Creator. I am, however, going to remember that it's not the only kind of beauty there is. Spiritual beauty also reflects back to the Creator and benefits many.

God gives so many different wonderful gifts to all of us. Looks, talent, intelligence – they all come from Him and none of us can take credit for them. To some He gives the ability to sing or write. Some of us excel in the visual arts. Some of us can run like the wind or dive off a high dive and enter the water like an arrow. Some of us are wonderful organizers and others of us know how to inspire others.

When we stop pining for what we don't have we can develop what we do have. Realizing that I was less than beautiful motivated me to develop something that, in the long run, stood me in good stead: personality. I developed my wit and love for fun. I made friends and I learned how to get along with people.

It finally sunk in that, although I wasn't beautiful, I wasn't completely unattractive, either. I was good enough looking to attract my adorable husband. He still thinks I'm cute and I love him for it.

It has been a lifelong process, but I'm coming to understand that God has blessed me beyond measure in giving me eyes that can see, ears that can hear (not as well as when I was thirty, but that's okay), and working limbs. That nose that I've never liked has served me well, allowing me to enjoy the fragrance of a rose and the aroma of baking cookies.

I often quote Proverbs 31:30 to myself: "Charm is deceptive and beauty is fleeting; but a woman who fears the LORD is to be praised." These days I try to remember to keep living a life that pleases God my number one priority. And I must say, as I focus on that it leaves me completely happy and satisfied.

Like Naomi at the end of her story, God has shone His light on my life. I can see myself as blessed. I have a wonderful family and great friends, all of whom have helped me through some very hard times. God has given me the gift of creativity and I've enjoyed seeing many of my stories turned into books and movies. God has forgiven me of all my sins and bad attitudes. He's showed me mercy and has wrapped me in His love. Like Naomi, I have been blessed. There is no need to carry around that old, negative name.

That's me. What about you? Perhaps you've had similar experiences to mine or to those of the women who shared with me. What negative name might you be carrying?

Let's keep this discussion going and talk about names we need to lose.

1. New International Version
2. New Living Translation
3. Ruth 1: 20, 21, New King James
4. New International Version
5. New International Version

FIVE
THE NAMES WE CALL OURSELVES

In the last chapter we discussed how our circumstances can affect the names we give ourselves and touched on how they can affect our self-image, our attitude toward life, and our behavior. Let's talk some more about those names we call ourselves and see what God has to say about them.

Mara (Bitter)

Maybe you use that as your last name. Maybe you preface it with I Deserve to Be.

It's so easy to let our circumstances turn us bitter. We often go into a situation with certain expectations: I'll get that job... Of course he'll fall in love with me ... my friend will never cheat me ... my children will grow up to honor me. When those expectations aren't met, we are disappointed, crushed, angry. And then bitter. Like Naomi was. And when that bitterness feels justified it can be hard to let go of it.

But bitterness breeds misery. Bitterness makes us hard and brittle. It not only colors the way we see our world, but it also affects the way we react to others. It repels rather than attracts and when our bitterness drives people away we compound our misery. Bitterness blinds us to the work of God in our lives.

That doesn't mean it's easy to resist taking that name when you're suffering. Maybe you're dealing with a severe handicap or auto immune disease or battling cancer. Maybe you've lost loved ones. Perhaps you've been fired or laid off. That can seem especially unfair.

If you're standing on the shore of bitter waters this might be a time to remember the story of Job. If anyone had a right to curse God, it was him. On top of losing everything he valued he lost the support of his friends. Even his wife gave up on him, advising him to "Curse God and die.[1] How's that for supportive?

Job could have blamed God, could have cursed his Creator for what was happening to him. He could have also blamed himself as his three friends urged him to do. *You must have done something, buddy. Fess up!* But he didn't. And he didn't follow his wife's advice to curse God, either. He did, however, wonder what on earth was going on.

If you're struggling through deep, dark waters right now you might be asking, "What bad thing did I do to bring this on myself?" Maybe, like Job, you didn't do anything.

When we were coping with how to help our handicapped daughter some well-meaning church members urged us to ask forgiveness for our sins because sin was why this terrible thing had happened to us. Once more the Bible verse God had implanted earlier in my mind and my heart came to mind. The book of John gives a biblical account of a man born blind. Jesus' disciples asked him what sin this man or his parents had committed that he had been cursed with blindness. We see his reply in John 9:3: "'Neither this man nor his parents sinned,' said Jesus, 'but this happened that the work of God might be displayed in his life.'"[2]

In that account the blind man was healed, but God did not provide a miraculous healing for our daughter. Still, I do hope that, over the years, people saw God at work in our lives. And maybe, as with that blind man and his family, people are seeing God at work in your life as you grapple with your own difficult circumstances.

The real culprit behind Job's suffering was Satan, who was out to destroy him. And why was that? Because Job was living an exemplary life, one that honored God. If there is anything evil hates, it's goodness.

For all you know, your walk with God has shone brightly enough to merit attack. If that's the case, your suffering is an honor, a spiritual merit badge. Just as God was able to turn those bitter waters sweet for the young nation of Israel, newly escaped from Egypt, so is He able to turn your bitterness to joy.

Like Job and Naomi, we often go through hard times with no idea why. But we may see later the why behind those times or at least the good that came out of them.

Right now, my dear friend Sarah is battling Parkinson's disease, a horrible neurodegenerative disorder that affects neurons in a specific area of the brain. There is no cure for it and the disease can afflict its sufferer with everything from tremors to slurred speech to difficulties swallowing. The disease itself is not fatal but its complications can be serious, and Sarah is dealing with many of them. But she says, "I still have my smile." She is an inspiration to me and many others.

Who might you be an inspiration to in your time of trouble? You may never know, but if you are keeping close to God, I guarantee you that you're inspiring someone.

We can't see what's happening in unseen realms, we can't know future outcomes of what we're experiencing, and we can't know for sure who's watching our story unfold or what influence we might have on someone either now or down the road.

We can, however, know that "...God causes everything to work together for the good of those who love God and are called according to his purpose for them."[3]

Every time I read about Job, and I can't help asking myself, "Why did God let Satan torture that poor man so much? Why didn't He tell Satan to bug off? What was the purpose of Job's suffering?" God doesn't tell us why exactly. But as we read about him, we can see that God had confidence that Job would hold up under pressure. Job's story shows countless generations down through the ages that we can survive whatever Satan throws at us. Perhaps that's why God allowed it. Job survived the evil attacks aimed at him. So will we.

When I think of all Job's sufferings, I'm most horrified over the loss of all his children. No parent wants to outlive a child. It's not the natural order of things. It amazes me that right then and there Job didn't shake his fist at God and cry, "I hate you!" Even though the loss of this life doesn't mean the end of our existence it's hard to lose those we love. And a child. Is there any greater grief?

The first shock wave of losing our handicapped daughter a few years ago was horrible. I mourned both the life she lost and the life she had missed out on. I grieved that now it was too late to do anything more for her, be anything more to her. I wept as I watched her coffin lowered into the ground. I still weep at the memory of it.

But God has enabled both myself and my husband to bypass the bitter waters of resentment. I don't need to name myself Mara because God is still with me, and my child is now with Him. My loss is not permanent. I will see my daughter again.

When our expectations clash with God's plans for us, when our dreams are thwarted by the actions of others it's important to remember that our lives are in God's hands, that whatever is happening to us is happening for a reason. We may not understand that reason, we may not be able to see the outcome of our current circumstances, but we can trust that God is working things out for good. Not simply our good.

You don't have to allow your current circumstances to define your identity. Remember, you're not simply going through something, you're *growing* through something for a reason. You are learning, you are gaining spiritual muscle, and you are possibly inspiring others. And if, as with Job, Satan has asked God for permission to attack you, know that, like Job, God is pleased with you ... and Satan will not be able to destroy you.

Negativity loves to attach itself to us and all it needs is one bad experience, one hurtful remark from someone we love and respect, one betrayal. But God can keep us from falling into bitterness if we keep our focus on Him and the sure knowledge that He is with us, no matter what and He cares for us. Our Lord knows how to walk on water. If you take His hand and keep looking to Him with every step, He won't let you sink.

If you've named yourself Mara and are ready to shed that name, ask God to help you see instances of His goodness in your life and commit to trusting Him with your future. Remember how God turned those bitter waters in the desert into sweet for the nation of Israel? He can also turn your bitterness into sweet fellowship. Just as He used wood to transform those waters, He has a special wood that will transform your outlook and attitude and that is the wood of the cross where Christ was crucified. When we turn to Him and accept the work that was done on that cross, when we ask Him to cure us of our bitterness and substitute peace and hope for it, He will turn us from bitter to sweet.

Now is the time to take Naomi's name and allow God to help you refocus. Just as the nation of Israel had to act on what

God had done and drink the improved water, you too, will have to act on what God has provided for your spiritual health. You will have to move forward with a new attitude and change your self-talk. Choose phrases that will clean out the bitterness, such as: If God is for me, who can be against me? Every day find one thing for which to be grateful. Maybe that is only one thing. Maybe it will be that same thing over and over again. That's okay. Don't lose sight of it. Know that God will enable you to grow into that new and better name.

Ugly

Perhaps, like me, this is a name you've carried. If so, I wouldn't be surprised. I've never met a woman who said, "I love everything about the way I look." Have you? I've heard, "My nose is too big," and "My breasts are too small." I've heard, "I hate my hair," ... "I wish I had curly hair," which is usually followed by someone saying, "No, you don't. You don't want my curly hair." (Since going through chemo and seeing myself with no hair I have ceased to complain about my stick-straight hair. Well, most of the time, anyway.)

Nose, hips, feet, you name it, we all manage to find fault with our appearance. We all, at one time or other, look in the mirror and wish we saw something different.

Our culture not only tells us we should be beautiful, but it also tells us how we should be beautiful. What it doesn't tell us is that all of us, in our own unique way, already are beautiful.

Perhaps you've compared yourself to other women and found yourself lacking. Perhaps you were teased as a child. Names like Fatty or Beanpole have stuck with you and followed you into your adult life. You were teased because you had a big nose or were growing a crop of pimples. If you wore glasses, you might have been called Four Eyes. Even worse, you might have been labeled with a racial slur that left you longing for a different skin color. Maybe your experiences as a child or teenager left you carrying around the idea that you are undesirable and undeserving of love. As I've showed in the previous chapter, even having someone in your life who loves you can't quite erase that off-kilter self-image.

How does this kind of name shaming play out? It makes you prey to every cosmetic and clothing ad on the planet, every promise of quick weight loss or wrinkle free skin, every procedure guaranteed to make you more beautiful. The last I checked the cosmetics industry was worth 93.5 billion dollars in the U.S.[4] I'm sure it's gone up since, and who knows what it will be by the time you read this book. One thing I think I can safely guarantee. The market won't have shrunk.

There's a reason for that. We women are constantly being propagandized to believe we are not good enough as we are. Only we don't call it propaganda. We call it marketing. If you buy into what you're told in the marketplace you can never be content with how you look, no matter what you do. You'll get one thing fixed and something new will present itself to whisper that name Ugly in your ear. You'll spend a fortune on makeup and clothes and still never be sure of yourself.

Men can fall prey to propaganda, also. Maybe not as hard as we women, but Satan likes to whisper insults in their ears, too. They're told they need pecs the size of a gorilla's along with a six-pack.

And they definitely need hair. Hair growth products abound on the shelves of the internet. Hair treatments, hair replacement. To many men, bald is a four-letter word. I get that. I didn't like my chem no-hair phase one little bit. We're designed to have hair. It keeps our heads warm. But, when the gene pool is playing dirty, when time marches on and hairlines recede this does not need to be cause for mourning.

It's important to remind our men of their good qualities. They need to know that, while God wants them (and us!) to keep those bodies in the best shape possible, their looks don't affect their value. The kind of strength that makes a man a true hero is spiritual strength. And the kind of beauty that makes a woman truly lovely? Same thing.

It's time for us to realize that our heavenly Father sees us all as beautiful creations. You doubt it? Let's see what the Bible has to say.

"God created man in His own image, in the image of God He created him; male and female He created them." – Genesis 1:27 [5]

Created in the image of God, we bear His stamp. How could you not be beautiful when you reflect the goodness and kindness of God?

Here's another verse, one you've probably read at some time or other.

"I will give thanks *and* praise to You, for I am fearfully and wonderfully made;
Wonderful are Your works,
And my soul knows it very well." – Psalm 139:14 [6]

Fearfully and wonderfully made. Don't you love the sound of that? We are all complex, thinking, feeling beings descended from an unfathomably long line of thinking feeling beings. We have bodies designed not only to work functionally so we can see, hear, smell, move and carry, but also so that we can smile and laugh and speak. Our bodies have been designed to fight off disease and heal when injured. And the heart inside that body – think of all the work it does, the never-ending beating for years and years, just to keep us going. And it all started with dirt. Amazing!

You may be thinking something very cynical right now, like, *Yeah, but you don't have my body*. Perhaps you have a disfiguring scar or are missing a limb. Maybe you're wheelchair bound.

Maybe you've battled breast cancer and lost a breast – a terribly hard thing for us women as our breasts are a part of our identity. Please know that your identity is so much larger than that part of your body. Those who love us understand that. In fact, those who love us see beyond all our imperfections.

It's what we do with the body we have that people really pay attention to. I recently saw a reel on Instagram of a cute young girl, dancing and doing some impressive leaps. And she had on such a cute outfit.

And she had no arms.

But what a smile. And what a lovely dancer she was. Not simply beautiful, but inspiring.

It is so important not to let what we have lost physically deprive us of what we own spiritually. The outer body, like the cars we drive, needs to be maintained but it's only the "vehicle" we get around in, and that vehicle will eventually wear out. The real us is so much more. We as women are more than our body parts. Our love, our example of godly living is what keeps our families strong.

The thing you see wrong about yourself might not be as dramatic as a disfiguring injury but is still just as upsetting to you. Let me give you another Scripture, a reminder of what is most important.

"Charm can mislead and beauty soon fades.
The woman to be admired and praised
is the woman who lives in the Fear-of-God."
– Proverbs 31:30 [7]

Let me reiterate, beauty is gift, and one we can all appreciate. But it's not a lasting one. I think of physical beauty as a gorgeous birthday cake – so lovely, so tasty... and soon gone. That cake is meant to be appreciated and enjoyed, but compare it to, say, a high-end digital camera or a smart phone you can use to take pictures of special occasions and favorite pets. Both are gifts for which we should thank the giver, but which one will last the longest? If you've been gifted with beauty, of course, be thankful. If you feel lacking in that area switch your focus and take stock of the other gifts God has given you. It's that simple. Maybe not that easy, but that simple.

When it comes to physical beauty, it's not, as the saying goes, a level playing field, but here's one area where the playing field is level: we all have access to the gift of God's grace and the Holy Spirit, and no matter what we look like on the outside we all can develop inner beauty. Inner beauty won't fade.

Here's good advice to keep in mind. "Don't be concerned about the outward beauty that depends on jewelry, or beautiful clothes, or hair arrangement. Be beautiful inside, in your hearts, with the lasting charm of a gentle and quiet spirit that is so precious to God." – 1 Peter 3:3,4 [8]

I'm not saying we should never again buy lipstick or mascara. Or cute shoes on sale.

Or a pretty dress. I'm sure, like me, you've had occasion to buy a dress that made you smile when you put it on. I still remember fondly one I bought when I was thirty. It was gorgeous – white taffeta with black polka dots, a sassy ruffled skirt, sweetheart neckline. Oh, my, did I feel like something in that dress.

But, in the end, it was only window dressing. Wrapping paper. What was real was what was inside that dress. Me. We all love a prettily wrapped present, but in the end, the present is what we concentrate on, not the wrapping.

So, we need to spend a fortune on clothes and makeup and expensive procedures to be truly, lastingly beautiful? No, we don't. And we don't have to compete with each other or with those images of air brushed models we see in magazine ads for perfume. When we serve God, when we are at peace with others, that is when we really shine.

You are unique and beautiful in God's eyes. I encourage you to reject the temptation to label yourself Ugly or Not Pretty, to bemoan whatever feature you hate next time you look in the mirror. It's a name that doesn't suit you.

Useless

The sad thing about this name is that, like a virus, it attaches itself to us when we are vulnerable, invading after a failure or disappointment. This can leave us feeling depressed, isolated and hopeless. When we buy into all this name implies, we give up on life. We shrug and say, "What's the point?"

The temptation to do this is especially strong when we get older. It can feel like the whole world is changing, moving in a new direction and leaving us behind. The music in church changes (including the decibel at which it's played). It seems like it's all geared for the younger generation. The pastor is young enough to be your son. The women's group always brings in younger speakers. You feel that you are old and no longer viable. And then there's the workplace. You may see younger employees eyeing your job. Perhaps you've experienced age discrimination. You're feeling irrelevant and a little left out at family gatherings.

Yes, things change, and the next generation steps up to take their place in the family, the workforce, the church. But that doesn't mean the older generation is no longer valuable. If you doubt that, read about Moses, who was no young man when he led the Israelites out of Egypt, or Abraham, who became a

father at the age of eighty-six.[9] Think of people like Grandma
Moses, who only became famous late in life.

No matter what your age, you matter. You may not have the
energy you had when you were thirty, but there is always something you can do. You can donate money to worthy causes and
write notes of encouragement. You can teach Sunday School or
mentor a younger woman, bake cookies for the neighbors, knit
or crochet blankets to donate to your local pregnancy care
center, open up your home for a Bible study, get politically
active and write your senator and congressperson. Or how
about texting encouraging quotes and Scripture to your grand-
children?

I think of my oldest brother, Ben. Sadly, our family lost him
a few years ago and we still feel the loss. He was eighty-two
when he died, but right up until his departure time he was
coaching basketball, involved in a men's Bible study, mowing
his daughter's lawn, and hosting our huge family gatherings.
Making a difference. My other big brother, Sam, and his wife
moved into a retirement home and became active right away.
They sing in a choir and do weekly grocery runs to stock the
small store in the facility, making themselves useful to their
fellow residents.

Age doesn't diminish our value and as long as we're here
there is something we can be doing to be useful. Even if your
health isn't good or your finances are limited that doesn't take
you off the team. You can still be an encourager. You can still
pray for others.

There is no such thing as useless in God's kingdom. If you
are still here, you're here for a reason. The older generation has
seen things, suffered things and learned things that the younger
ones haven't. You have life experiences and wisdom from
which others can benefit. Long life is a blessing and age

demands respect. God even commanded that His people respect their aged.[10]

If you're feeling like you've been put out to pasture and nobody cares, I hope the following Bible verses will inspire you.

"Is not wisdom found among the aged? Does not long life bring understanding?"

– Job 12:12 [11]

"The righteous will flourish like a palm tree, they will grow like a cedar of Lebanon; planted in the house of the Lord, they will flourish in the courts of our God. They will still bear fruit in old age, they will still stay fresh and green, proclaiming, 'The LORD is upright; he is my Rock and there is no wickedness in him.'"

– Psalm 92: 12-15 [12]

"So we do not give up. Our physical body is becoming older and weaker, but our spirit inside us is made new every day." – 2 Corinthians 4:16 [13]

Remember the days of old, consider the years long past; ask your father, and he will inform you;

your elders, and they will tell you. - Deuteronomy 32:7 [14]

"The glory of young men is their strength, gray hair the splendor of the old."

– Proverbs 20:29 [15]

I love these verses! (Especially the last one, considering the color of my hair now.) Maybe, after reading them, you're going to want to give yourself a new name. Wise Woman? Highly Valued? Or maybe, in light of the last verse, Splendid.

Aging isn't the only thing that can make us feel useless. Any life change can leave us feeling unwanted and despondent. Let's talk for a moment about a change in roles. For many of us women, empty-nest syndrome is a very real and painful thing. Even though our goal as parents is to raise our children to become that separate entity known as a responsible adult, seeing this play out can cause emotional turmoil. For many years that child needed us, depended on us. Suddenly the chick is off to college or moving out and we're left with a void. Questions arise. Who needs me now? Who am I? What am I to do with the rest of my life?

There will always be someone somewhere who needs what you have to offer. You are a composite – mother, daughter, friend, worker, church member. What else? Baker? Musician? Artist? Writer? Athlete? Coach? Teacher? Encourager? As for what to do with the rest of your life, ask God. He will open doors, help you find new interests and develop talents long-neglected. You, like your children, are maturing and growing and God will lead you down new life paths.

If you have been a caregiver to a parent or spouse, the loss of that person can leave you asking those same questions, wondering what you do with all that time suddenly hanging on your hands. Your mourning is compounded because in addition to losing that person who meant so much to you, you have lost your identity as a caregiver. If you are a born caregiver, believe that God will give you other opportunities to reach out and help others.

A job loss or a career cut short can be devastating as well. Again, the question that arises is, "Who am I now?" You are a daughter of God, and He has plans for you. Count on it.

Our roles and job assignments change throughout our lives, so don't lose sight of the fact that your identity is much more than any one role you play at any given time. Remember, we are all servants of God, and in His kingdom every servant has a job to do and a reason for being there, serving the King. The way God uses you throughout your life will change, but He will never consider you useless.

Nobody

Have you opted for a variation of this name, such as Less Than or Not Good Enough? The problem with these names is we can exhaust ourselves trying to ditch them. We say yes to everyone who wants something from us, we sacrifice relationships and rest while frantically working to reach the top of the ladder of success. We try to be mini-gods crowned with wealth and success or we try to be paragons of sacrifice, being all things to all people. Our relationship with God is one of constant striving, trying to finally deserve His love, forgetting that He loved us before we ever loved him.[16] He was willing to die for us when we were still sinners.[17]

The flip side of that is just as bad. We give up and live with those names. We don't volunteer for anything because, after all, we won't measure up. So what's the point? It's a muddy slope we put our feet on when we think like this, and we can only slide further down it into the muck of resentment and bitterness.

I hear the term low self-esteem a lot. I think of this more in terms of not understanding or appreciating what God has given us and where He's placed us. Maybe we should instead call this problem low gift esteem.

Remember, we all have gifts and talents. That means we all have a purpose. Sadly, our culture both outside and inside the church glorifies the "sexy" gifts. We turn athletes and actors into celebrities. We admire writers and idolize singers. In the church most of us want to be teachers or preachers or to be on the worship team. Those ministries seem to get the attention.

But we are all part of the body of Christ, and our goal isn't to glorify ourselves, it's to glorify Him. Simply being part of something so hugely important to the human race means our lives matter, and any service, great or small is of value to our Lord. I like to think of the parable of the widow's mite that we read about in both Mark 12 and Luke 21. In this parable, a poor widow offered a seemingly insignificant gift to God, and yet God valued it highly because she gave all she had to give.

The apostle Paul deals with this issue of value in his first letter to the Corinthians. You can find his discourse in the twelfth chapter, where he reminds believers that, just like a physical body, the church, known as the body of Christ, is made up of many parts. Nobody gets to say to anybody, "You are not important," because every single part is needed for the body to function effectively. Verse 27 says, "Now you are the body of Christ, and each one of you is a part of it."[18]

After this verse, he goes on to list some of the parts of the body of the early church, starting with the apostles and preachers and teachers. But he doesn't stop there. He lists those with a gift of healing, those who can organize and administrate, those who have a gift for helping.

Even if you're not a CEO of a large corporation, a surgeon or a senator, an actor, a songwriter, an astronaut, or a bishop, you still have a unique place in God's kingdom. Everyone matters to someone. If you're someone's child you're important to that parent. If you're someone's parent, you are needed by that child. If you're someone's sibling or friend, you're an important part of the fabric of that person's life. If you're a teacher, you are helping shape young minds. If you're an architect, a builder, a truck driver, a flagger or a landscaper or a factory worker, you are contributing to life's big picture, and are as important to that picture as every brush stroke is to the painting an artist creates.

Every single gift and talent each of us possesses is needed for all of us to function well together as a group of believers. Your prayers are needed for those you love and for your pastor, for your local community leaders, definitely for those leading our nation. Your muscles are needed when there's a call for people to come help clean the church or weed the flowerbeds. Your creativity is appreciated when it's time to decorate the church for the holidays. When a family is going through a crisis or has a parent in the hospital the last thing they want to think about is meal preparation, and your culinary skills are needed. They are definitely appreciated when it comes time for that coffee hour after church. If you volunteer in the church office, if you're a greeter, if you're keeping the bathrooms cleaned, you are just as vital as the person at the front of the church playing the piano or singing. (If you don't believe that, imagine someone's reaction when that person goes to use the bathroom and finds no toilet paper in the stalls.)

Chances are your skills and talents will also be appreciated in your community. Volunteers are a dying breed and organizations always appreciate help. Maybe you're needed to work in your local food bank or organize a neighborhood watch program or help out at your children's school. Do you have organizational gifts? How about helping organize a ladies night out for your local businesses? Or simply serving on the committee. Politicians always need someone to go door belling or put up signs.

Maybe it's time for you to start your own business. I think of my friend Laura, who started her organic soap company F.R.O.G Soap. She's doing something she loves – recycling oil and providing eco-friendly products. Purpose Boutique, a clothing store in my area is about more than purpose. Its founder and CEO Christie Johnson used her gift for style for more than business. A percentage of every sale goes to fight human trafficking. They also offer over twenty brands created by survivors of trafficking around the world. These are just two examples of women who recognized their gift and decided to pursue and develop it.

Then there's you. What gift have you been ignoring or

minimizing while wishing for something you think is more important? What could you be doing with that gift? Is there an organization in need of it? Do you have a business idea you'd like to pursue? Think outside the box (or inside it). Ask God to open your eyes and show you where He wants you. He will.

We are all servants of Christ and there's no such thing as a super star in God's kingdom. There's also no such thing as a useless person. If you've been hauling around the name Useless dump it. Because the name itself is far more useless than you will ever be.

Stupid

Is this a name you were called growing up? Perhaps you have dyslexia and reading has always been difficult for you. Perhaps, you were never good at math. Or spelling. You may have translated that particular deficiency into an overall lack of mental ability.

Let me tell you right now, if you are seeking God, you are far from stupid. Intellect, like beauty, is from God. Some of us may have a larger portion than others of us, but whether your portion is big or small, God can use you. He can give you something even more important than smarts. He can give you wisdom.

Wisdom is much more important than intellectual prowess because it goes a step beyond and sees through God's eyes. I don't know about you, but I've known a lot of smart people who excel at making stupid decisions.

Proverbs 9:10 tells us that wisdom begins with fearing God, acknowledging what a powerful Being our Creator is. This kind of wisdom is available to us all. Proverbs 2:6 tells us that it is the Lord who gives wisdom. That means we all have access to it and, according to James 1:5, all we have to do is ask for it.

That being the case, does it really matter if you weren't at the top of your class? Does God care if you are a lousy speller. These days we have computers to fix our bad spelling.

A relative of mine often bragged about how smart her children and grandchildren are, but when it came to herself that was a different story. The last time we were visiting, and she called herself stupid I asked her what made her think she was stupid. It was a mystery to me because this woman is far from it.

"I don't have a college degree," she said. In her mind no college degree equals no smarts.

Education is a good thing. For many it's the ticket out of poverty. Educating ourselves on issues enables us to make wise decisions. Reading skills expand our horizons. But all the degrees in the world will prove useless if we ignore the One who created us and fail to learn from Him.

Are you lacking a higher education and feeling like that missing diploma means you don't measure up? If you are, you're using the wrong measuring stick. Further your education if it's needed for your job. Further it if you want to know more about a particular subject or if you simply love learning. But don't look for a degree to confirm your worth as a person.

Having said that, I understand how being around highly educated people can feel intimidating. My best friend is brilliant and teaches gifted kids. Her husband has multiple degrees. So does my husband. Then there's little old me, who never finished college. (*All those math and science classes I still have to take? Never mind. I'll choose a different path.*)

I remember a time when, being with these three, I felt like the dim bulb in the box. But I eventually came to realize that a different intelligence is not an inferior intelligence. I have been gifted with creativity, which is an intelligence all its own. I don't have to have multiple degrees to be of use to God and I don't have to win at Trivial Pursuit to feel good about myself.

Most important, I have a vast mine of heavenly wisdom at my disposal. Over the years, as I worked that mine, my feelings of intellectual inferiority vanished. I no longer wish I am "as smart as." Instead, I'm grateful for all I've learned from studying my Bible. I know my worth in Christ.

Do you know your worth in Christ? Are you going to that mine of godly wisdom and grabbing those nuggets of gold? Please know that this is where true and lasting wisdom can be found. If you are seeking God, you are far from stupid. You are wise.

Before we move on, let me just say that all this is not to downplay intelligence. You might have been teased about this gift, called names like Nerd and Teacher's Pet. Do you have a child who's being teased because that extra dose of smarts makes the child stick out when all he or she wants to do is blend in? It's okay to remind both your child and yourself that diamonds don't blend in.

Go ahead and sparkle... for the Lord. When you give your intelligence to God, He will bring ways for you to use it for Him, whether it's teaching, writing, or witnessing to someone (who is equally intelligent and needs to talk with a believer who is skilled in apologetics).

Whatever your level of education, however smart you think you are or aren't, always keep in mind that the fountainhead of wisdom is the fear of the Lord, respecting, honoring and acknowledging His awesome power. This is true intelligence. And yes, if you are following Him, you have it.

Abandoned

There are times when we feel alone in our struggles. Is this where you are? If so, read these words of King David:

> "My God, my God, why have you forsaken me?
> Why are you so far from saving me,

So far from my cries of anguish?
My God, I cry out by day, but you do not answer,
By night, but I find no rest." [19]

Our Lord, on the cross, quoted from this Psalm. He was rejected by his people and abandoned by His disciples. He understands what you are feeling.

Abandonment is a tragic byproduct sinful behavior in our fallen world. It causes us to see ourselves through a lens created, not by God, but by others.

A child given up for adoption may feel this even if the adopted parents love that child very much. Why? Because the first person in the child's life left him or her. *The person who gave me life didn't care enough about me to share it.* There can be valid reasons for why a parent gave up a child, but the child only sees the action and not the motivation.

Someone whose spouse has left the marriage is also going to feel abandoned. *Once someone was in my life, now that person doesn't want to be with me.* The evidence is there. It's obvious and it's painful. Even losing a spouse or parent to death can feel like an abandonment. *That person was there for me, my biggest cheerleader. Now who is left that will care as much?*

This is what our senses and our emotions see. What is harder to determine is what's happening in the unseen world, the one where our God works on our behalf, where He sees and weeps over us. How can we apply the unseen to what is before our physical eyes, to what has happened in our physical world?

We must have faith. We must take that first step by resolving that we will look beyond what is evident in the physical world. We must pray, "Lord, I am going to trust that You are with me even though I can't see You working or feel your presence. Even though I have been abandoned by someone here in the earthly realm, you are still with me." We next tell ourselves, "I know what it looks like, but God has not abandoned me."

Why would He? He loves us. This doesn't mean we won't experience pain though. It doesn't mean that others won't hurt us or leave us. It doesn't mean we won't have to struggle.

Think of times your children have had to struggle, maybe been hurt by friends. Oh, my, I can think of times when other girls hurt my daughter. I wanted to step in and rip off their cute, little freckled faces. But much as I tried to protect her, there were times when I couldn't. There were situations she had to cope with on her own. It broke my heart.

If you are a parent, I bet you've gone through similar circumstances. We'd like nothing better than to wrap our children in a safe little bubble, so they'll never experience hurt.

That doesn't stop once they reach adulthood. Their hurts are our hurts. Like my mother once said, "You never stop being a parent."

Surely it grieves God equally to see us, His children, suffer. But, sadly, hurt is part of this fallen world filled with broken people who misuse the free will they were given. It finds our children, and it finds us all sooner or later. That doesn't mean our heavenly Father isn't there with us, ready to comfort and strengthen us.

The apostle Paul said, "We are hard pressed on every side, but not crushed, perplexed, but not in despair, persecuted, but not abandoned, struck down, but not destroyed." [20] This from a man who was beaten, stoned, shipwrecked and imprisoned. If ever a man had the right to feel abandoned, it was Paul. I look at his words and say to myself, "Surely, if God was with Paul in everything, he went through He will be with me as well." There may be times when I am perplexed over what's happening to me, but there will never be a time when God abandons me.

Here's a great verse to quote to yourself when you are feeling abandoned and no longer equal to the task of coping:

"I lift up my eyes to the hills – from where will my help come?
My help comes from the LORD, who made heaven and earth."
Psalm 121:1,2 [21]

We can (and should) love and commit to people. Sometimes we can even depend on people. But ultimately, our hope lies in our Lord. He alone will remain with us no matter what. He won't die, He won't disappoint.

Let me remind you, Jesus promised His disciples that He would not leave them orphaned.[22] He left them physically, but He sent His Holy Spirit, which empowered them to do great things in His name. He won't leave us orphaned either, no matter who else may forsake us. We can count on this because the evidence of His faithfulness is recorded in Scripture.

No matter what your circumstances, no matter what you feel, you are not abandoned by the One who matters most of all. You are watched over. You are ... Protected.

Unwanted/Unloved

Maybe you never felt wanted by your parents. They never left physically but they never filled the emotional well either. Or perhaps you were that child on the playground who was teased or ignored, always picked last when choosing teams, overlooked when the birthday party invitations went out.

People are fickle and their loyalty can disappear faster than chips at a party. People's brokenness can prevent them from reaching out in love. When that happens, they break more people.

You may have been broken and wound up looking for love in relationships that always disappointed you. In that search to be loved you may have done things you now regret. But the good news is that you are loved by God, and His love never fails.

A favorite verse we often hear quoted can be found in the book of Jeremiah, chapter 29:11: "'I know the plans I have for you,' declares the LORD, plans to prosper you and not to harm you, plans to give you hope and future.'"[23] That sure sounds like love to me!

In another verse we see God scolding His people, the nation of Israel, through the prophet Jeremiah. But even though they were being disciplined, Jeremiah reminded this wayward nation of how much God loved them, had always loved them. "The LORD appeared to us in the past, saying: 'I have loved you with an everlasting love; I have drawn you with loving-kindness...'"[24]

As followers of Christ, we've been added to that group of beloved people. We each matter to God. If you doubt that, read John 3:16. God's love is big enough to encompass the entire world. He created us and He wants us for His very own. That is the ultimate in being wanted.

People fall in and out of love, but God's love for us is constant. If you struggle with feeling unloved, Romans 8:38, 39 might be good to memorize. "For I am persuaded that neither death nor life, nor angels nor principalities nor powers, nor things present nor things to come, nor height nor depth, nor any other created thing, shall be able to separate us from the love of God which is in Christ Jesus our Lord."[25]

Those who have grown up with us may not understand us. Those we work with may not appreciate us. Those who call us friends may drift out of our lives or, even worse, turn on us. A spouse's love may wane, children might ignore us, but the One who created us will always love us and will always be there for us. When we turned to His Son, He adopted us, and He, unlike earthy parents, is a perfect Father who works all things together

for our good. You may feel unloved, but if you are a follower of
Christ, you can rest assured that you are not. You are loved
with an everlasting love.

Unforgivable

This name leads only to despair and recklessness. Yet how
many of us have adopted it at some time or other?

Have you ever felt this should be your name? Do past sins
and mistakes haunt you, making you depressed or afraid? I
confess, I often think about things I've said and done and want
to weep. And the thought of standing before God one day... I
don't even like to go there.

But, having repented of those things I've done wrong (asked
forgiveness for and turned away from them) I can reject that
name and I can look to the day when I meet my Maker free of
fear because I have been forgiven. If you've repented, so
are you.

And yet, and yet.... Just as he did in the Garden of Eden,
the tempter comes alongside us and starts working on us. Just as
he asked Eve, "Did God really say...?" he will ask us, "Are you
sure those Bible verses apply to you?"

If you have surrendered to Christ as Lord and asked
forgiveness, then yes, they do. You can claim I John 1:9: "If we
confess our sins, He is faithful and just to forgive us our sins
and to cleanse us from all unrighteousness."[26] Cleansing means
we are no longer dirty. That unrighteousness is gone, washed
away by the blood of Jesus.

Here's another great Scripture to meditate on, Romans
4:24, 25. Here it is in the Amplified Bible translation:

"...[Righteousness, standing acceptable to God] will be granted
and accredited to us who believe (trust in, adhere to, rely on)
God, Who raised Jesus our Lord form the dead Who was
betrayed *and* put to death because of our misdeeds and was

raised to secure our justification (our acquittal), [making our account balance and absolving us from all guilt before God]."

I have this written on a notecard that I use as a bookmark in whatever book I happen to be reading. Every time I open that book, I start by reading the words on that card. What a comfort. I have been given standing acceptable to God. Jesus was put to death for my misdeeds (horrible!) but then raised to secure my justification and acquittal (amazing!) I have been acquitted and so have you. Remember, "... if anyone is Christ he is a new creation; the old has gone, the new has come!"[27]

Because we acknowledge who Jesus is we are forgiven we can have confidence that God's love is at work in our lives. We are not estranged, and the following verse proves it.

"If anyone acknowledges that Jesus is the Son of God, God
lives in him and he in God. And so we know and rely on the
love God has for us. God is love. Whoever lives in love lives in
God, and God in him. In this way love is made complete among
us so that we will have confidence on the day of judgement,
because in this world we are like him. There is no fear in
love..."
– 1 John 4:15-18 [28]

Not every person in your life may be able to forgive you for things you've done wrong, but God is more than able. He has forgiven you, and you can live in His love. So discard that negative name. Right now!

Unworthy

Satan loves to remind us of how very undeserving we are of God's grace and goodness. We look at our past sins or our bad attitudes and, instead of remembering that we're forgiven, we feel guilty. We see our flaws and feel unworthy of God's calling on our lives, unequal to the task of carrying out the plans He has for us. We sometimes even sabotage our own success by not getting out there and working to make those dreams God planted in our hearts come true because, deep down, we believe we don't deserve to succeed.

Let me tell you, if we were living by a merit system, then no one would be worthy of God's kindness. None of us can measure up to His standards of righteousness.

But God's love sees beyond that. His grace has been given to us even though none of us deserved it. And once you turn your life over to His Son, you move into a whole new territory, the land of Love. You become a child of God. God's love demonstrates that He sees the worth in you, that He saw it long before you ever did.

When Satan whispers in my ear, "Your name really should be Unworthy," I can reply with I John 3:1: "How great is the love the Father has lavished on us, that we should be called children of God!"[29] God deemed us worth His love, and He lavishes it on us. You have value because you are His.

Fearful

Do you carry this name around? Are you a Fanny Fearful? This can often go hand in hand with the conviction that we are not forgiven. It is often a result of only seeing God as stern and cruel, ready to strike you down for any mishap.

Yes, God is righteous and yes, like any good parent He disciplines us and allows us to experience both the good and bad of life. But, according to Ezekiel 33:11, He doesn't delight in punishing us any more than we delight in having to punish our own children. He only disciplines us because He wants what's best for us, and what's best for us is to live in close relationship with Him. A God who guides and disciplines us is not to be feared, and Hebrews 4:14-16 reminds us that because of all Jesus has done for us we can approach God with confidence, knowing we will receive mercy.

Fear for our safety or the safety of those we love can also prey on our minds. Simply watching the news rarely leaves us feeling calm because news is rarely good. Headlines announce catastrophes regularly. Social media is rife with news of the latest awful happening. You see wickedness everywhere and wonder what will become of our country and how you and your loved ones will be affected. You read about riots and violence and worry that they will reach your door and endanger your family. A constant barrage of negativity hardly makes for a calm spirit.

You may worry about finances (especially if you or your spouse has lost a job). We depend on those paychecks and most of live beyond our means, which means trouble if our source of income dries up. A fear of job loss is really a fear of losing the ability to pay the bills and keep a roof over our heads.

Health is another area of concern for many of us. I can understand this. Diseases like cancer are terrifying. And if you don't have good health insurance the worry of how you'll pay for treatment gets piled on top of the concern over whether or not you will survive.

Psalm 37:7-9 is good to read when you're feeling fearful.

Be still before the LORD and wait patiently for him; do not fret when men succeed in their ways, when they carry out their wicked schemes. Refrain from anger and turn from wrath, do not fret – it leads only to evil. For evil men will be cut off, but those who hope in the LORD will inherit the land."[30]

Fretting is a byproduct of fear. And it leads to evil? How so? What kind of evil?

For one thing, it undermines our trust in God, which is definitely not good. It says, "God can't handle this. He can't provide for your needs. He can't help you figure things out. He can't protect you."

It magnifies problems and feeds fear. Fear robs us of peace of mind and confidence. It often spurs us to rash, ill-considered and even illegal behavior. We take matters into our own hands and flail about. Fretting puts us on edge and can make us lash out at those we love. It says, "I don't trust God."

God has called us to walk in confidence and peace. Fearful is a name from the past. Bury that name and allow God to give you a new name fitting for a bold, spiritual fighter. When you're tempted to reclaim that name, dig into your Bible and claim Romans 8:37. You are a conqueror!

Failure

Here's a popular name, one we christen ourselves with when our plans don't succeed. If we hang onto that name, we will inherit the misery that comes with it. Seeing ourselves as failures can only lead to depression and discourage us from picking up and starting over, from assessing what went wrong and fixing it, from asking for and accepting forgiveness and moving on.

We all fail at something some time or other. Often those fails are small, like missing a friend's birthday or losing a competition. Sometimes they're huge and we wind up mourning the loss of a marriage or a job.

But making mistakes, making poor choices, committing sins – they are part of life. Isaiah 53:6 reminds us that, like lost sheep, we've all gone astray at some point. We make mistakes and we learn from them. When we are willing to re-start God can take us on to better things.

We'll talk more about this later, but for now keep in mind the fact that God gives beauty for ashes and turns failures into successes. Failing does not make you a failure.

NEGATIVE NAMES DO none of us any good, and whether they are names we give ourselves or names others try to push on us, we need to reject them. We also need to consider the source. Has someone called you a name in anger? Has someone who is jealous of you called you a name? Has that great deceiver, Satan, whispered a name in your ear? Resist the temptation to listen. Tell him you are a child of God and to scram.

Negative names have no place in God's kingdom or in our lives. We can shed them like a snake sheds its old skin. We need to leave them behind and walk away because God has much better names for us.

Beloved

He loves His people with an everlasting love. He bought them back from sin and death at the cost of His Son's life. Remember I John 3:1! God has lavished His love on you. He has not and will not abandon you. This is a name you have every right to claim for yourself.

Temple

Think what of all the labor that goes into the construction of a temple, the expense not spared. Read in the Old Testament about how much work and what cost went into building the temple in Jerusalem. And yet what temple does God inhabit? Us. We are the temple of the Holy Spirit[31]

Hopeful

According to Romans 5:1 we stand in grace and have the hope of glory. According to Ephesians 1:18 we have hope of an amazing inheritance. By the way, that verse also tells us that we have had the eyes of our hearts opened. We have been enlightened. Hmmm. Maybe you might want to start calling yourself Enlightened.

Wise

Remember that the fear of the Lord is the beginning of wisdom. As a child of God you have access to that wisdom. You have chosen to put your trust in His Son Jesus and to follow after Him. That makes you one smart cookie!

Lovely

Because, again, you belong to God. You have an inner beauty that will last clear through this life and into eternity. You are beautiful in God's sight. And, in the end, His opinion about your looks is the one that matters.

GOOD NAMES GIVE us something to live up to. But negative, defeating ones can serve no purpose. Still, we let people label us with them. We need to stop that.

Negative names can be changed when we turn to God and allow Him to work in our hearts, minds, and lives. We are made in the image of God. Let's claim that and live up to it. Whatever negative name you've been calling yourself, you have my permission to throw it off right now. Something better awaits.

1. Job 2:9
2. John 9:3, New International Version
3. Romans 8:28, New Living Translation
4. https://loudcloudhealth.com/beauty-industry-statistics/
5. New American Standard Bible
6. Amplified Bible
7. The Message
8. The Living Bible
9. Genesis 16:16
10. Leviticus 19:32

11. New International Version
12. New International Version
13. New Century Version
14. New International Version
15. New International Version
16. 1 John 4:19
17. Romans 5:8
18. New International Version
19. Psalm 22: 1, 2 New International Version
20. 2 Corinthians 4:8,9, New International Version
21. New International Version
22. John 14:18
23. Jeremiah, New International Version
24. Jeremiah 31: 3, New International Version
25. New King James translation
26. New King James translation
27. 2 Corinthians 5:17
28. New International Version
29. New International Version
30. New International Version
31. I Corinthians 6:19, 20

SIX
WHAT WAS YOUR NAME AGAIN?

Our names and our life stories are subject to change. Sometimes God gives us an entirely new name. Sometimes we forget who we are and have to be reminded. Here are some examples of how God works and reworks in and through His people. Whether your story begins poorly or starts well and takes a turn for the worse – either way our Creator knows your true identity.

Naomi, who we keep encountering, is such a great example of how names don't have to stick. Our human parents name us, friends and family give us nicknames, but the names that really count are the ones God gives us.

Each one of us has a unique story. That story will take many twists and turns before it ends. We will enjoy the view from the mountaintop and slide down into the valley. We will rest beside quiet waters and we'll trudge through the desert. We will feel blessed and be tempted to name ourselves Cursed. In all of this, God will be with us, watching over us.

I love the prophet Isaiah's message to the nation of Israel in the 61st chapter of his book in the Bible. Let me quote you some verses from the New International Version, starting with the very first one: "The Spirit of the Sovereign Lord is on me, because the Lord has anointed me to preach good news to the poor. He has sent me to bind up the brokenhearted, to proclaim freedom for the captives and release from darkness for the prisoners."

Talk about a much-needed positive message. Isaiah, whose name means the LORD Saves, wrote during a time when the Assyrian empire was on the rise and Israel was in decline.[1] If ever there was a time when God's people needed to be reminded that the LORD Saves it was then. Isaiah warned of upcoming disaster and punishment for sin, but in addition to that, he also predicted restoration and reminded the people of God's love for them. Isaiah saw repentance under King Hezekiah and rebellion under the kings who followed after. He alternately scolded and encouraged. And he warned. *Punishment is coming.*

He also reminded God's people that a time of healing would follow that punishment. Captives would be freed, and broken hearts mended. He also said in verse three that God had sent him to predict, "the year of the LORD'S favor and the day of vengeance of our God to comfort all who mourn, and provide for those who grieve in Zion – to bestow on them a crown of beauty instead of ashes, the oil of gladness instead of mourning and a garment of praise instead of a spirit of despair..."

The torn garments and ashes that signified mourning would be replaced with joy. So it is with us. We may feel abandoned, we may name ourselves Forgotten, but we never are. In the end, we come back to the true name God has for us: Beloved.

If you've made choices that have sent you in a wrong direction God can help you reverse direction. It's never too late to rethink priorities and change attitudes.

Hardship also has its place in our life story. It can both strengthen us and point us toward God. Hardship can be the soil that grows greatness.

I think of Joni Erickson Tada, who was paralyzed and wheelchair bound after a diving accident when she was only seventeen. Talk about having a reason to rename herself Mara! This woman has been an inspiration and help to countless people as an author and speaker and through her organization Joni and Friends, which not only gives help to people impacted by disability but shares the good news about Jesus. Would she have gone on to do all this without that horrible accident? Of course, we can't know. We can, however, know that God has worked in and through her life, turning around her hardship and suffering into something noble and bigger than herself.

God can work in our unhappiness and disappointment. He can change our life story and turn disaster to triumph. He can take a life in ruins and make it count for something.

When I was diagnosed with uterine cancer in 2013, the temptation to name myself Mara just as Naomi had done. was certainly strong. Other names came to mind: Stricken, Washed-Up, Ugly (yes, that again!). I traveled between mountaintop and valley on a regular basis, sometimes buoyant and close to the Lord, other times in despair, sometimes brave, other times terrified. Sometimes I was upbeat, other times cranky. Bald was not a good look for me and I avoided my mirror. Unless I was in the shower I was never without my wig or my sleeping cap. And after my hysterectomy I looked like the bride of Frankenstein, swollen and stitched. Surgery left me scarred and in pain, chemo often left me weak. I would not wish that that journey on anyone, but it did bring blessing. I was wrapped in love by family and friends and came to see how very loved I am. And I found a new name: Useful. I journaled my experience and published a memoir to encourage other women fighting the same battle.[2] Journaling gave each day a purpose and helped put my focus on what God wanted me to learn rather than my troubles. I had no idea what my future held, but my present held God as God held me.

If you are enduring hardship, take heart. What you're going through individually could very well be having an impact on both other believers and non-believers. As you walk through the fire, trusting God, you could be inspiring someone else to do the same. Your fight might also be offering someone an opportunity to exercise generosity and kindness by helping you. We are a body, and we function together to glorify God. We do this thing called life together, sharing and caring. Your need may be providing an opportunity for growth for someone else.

Suffering isn't the only thing that can define us. Past sins have a way of misshaping our perception of ourselves. Even when we know we are forgiven, it's easy to look back at bad choices and the fallout that came with them and think that is the final sum of who we are. We look at disappointments in the past and tend to want to drag them into the future.

That doesn't have to be the case. Our identity in Christ is much bigger than our past sins and problems. As with Naomi, God's plans trump ours. In the end, it is His name for us that matters. Let's look at some great examples of this from the Bible.

Moses the Murderer

We've already met Moses, one of the greatest heroes of the Bible. As you may know, it wasn't always that way. As you read his story it's easy to see that God had His hand on Moses's life from the very beginning. His early life and early failure are chronicled in the first two chapters of the book of Exodus.

He was born at a time when no parents of a male infant

were announcing, "It's a boy!" The Israelites had become a slave nation, but their number was increasing and their masters were beginning to fear what might happen if they revolted. Population control at its most brutal seemed the perfect solution and Pharaoh ordered all baby boys to be killed.

Not only did the baby Moses survive that awful time, but he wound up getting adopted by Pharaoh's daughter. Talk about an auspicious beginning.

But Moses made a huge misstep when he tried to help one of his own people by killing the Egyptian who was beating the man. He had to flee and that was the end of the life of privilege for Moses and, one would have thought, the end of his influence. He wound up exiled in the land of Midian, located in Southeastern Sinai – a dry and desolate land. How symbolic! He was there for forty years.[3]

And yet, look what happened. God brought him out of obscurity and he wound up leading his people to freedom. To this day he was one of the greatest heroes in Hebrew history.

Could God have raised up someone else to deliver His people? Of course, He could. But He didn't. Obviously, He had chosen Moses for this task, and when Moses's time of solitude and contemplation and, probably character growth, was at an end, God put him back in action.

It was a long wait. Moses could have given himself any number of names during that time, the chief one being Murderer. I'm betting there were also many days when he labeled himself a failure. Going from privilege to obscurity sure looks like failure. It's easy to see from all his objections once God laid out His plan for Moses how insecure this man felt. His first reaction was, "Who am I, that I should go to Pharaoh and bring the Israelites out of Egypt?"[4]

God knew who Moses was and who he could become. He had saved this man as a baby and preserved his life. He had been refining Moses and preparing him all along for this moment. Moses's story is a great example of how God can turn the course of a life when that person draws near to Him.

Samson the Big, Strong Brat

Samson is a good example of what happens when we ignore the name God has for us and our calling as His daughters. His birth was announced by an angel so surely his life should have had been gloriously heroic. According to my study Bible, his name is derived from the Hebrew word which means sun or brightness. His mother, infertile before his arrival, surely picked this name to describe the joy this baby brought to her.

Sadly, Samson didn't grow up to be one of those kids whose parents bragged about, saying, "He's been nothing but a joy."

He was, in fact, a trial from the very beginning, prideful, spoiled, and always falling for the wrong girl. If you want to read the whole story of Samson, you can find it in the Bible in the book of Judges, chapters thirteen through sixteen.

His amazing strength qualified him to be a hero of the young nation Israel, a leader and inspiration during a time when the country was struggling against the nation of Philistia. He did, indeed, create havoc among the Philistines, but when we think of Samson what do we think of? Haircuts.

Instead of resisting the enemy, he often fraternized with them. In contrast, the Philistine woman he fell for had no lack of loyalty to her people. Delilah was Samson's downfall, and his silliness when she'd beg him for the secret of his great strength shows pride and lack of respect for the gift God gave him.

I recently re-read his story, and seeing his conversations with Delilah, I'd find myself shaking my head and asking, "Were you the stupidest man on the planet or what? Did you honestly think she was interested in you?" Maybe he was simply the most conceited man on the planet, so impressed with his own gift that He forgot Who had given it to him.

Finally, he told her the truth. He was a Nazarite and to cut his hair would be to lose his strength. Perhaps, he, himself, didn't really believe that whole Nazarite vow thing. Perhaps he thought, Hey, I'm Samson, I'm indestructible. For sure he didn't grasp the importance of his calling or the true source of his strength.

It's easy to judge Samson. What a fool. What a narcissist! Why didn't he get it? But then I think about times I've relied on my own strength and realize I've had my Samson moments. Perhaps you have also.

Samson's foolishness cost him dearly. He was captured and blinded and shackled, set to work grinding grain in prison. A very ignoble end. Almost.

Samson begged for a chance to redeem himself and God granted it. Lo and behold, along came a big party, a swanky government function for the Who's Who of Philistia. When the party got a little dull the celebrants had a great idea. *Let's bring in blind, defeated Samson and mock him and gloat over our victory.*

Here was Samson's chance to redeem himself and we see his story ending as epically as it began, with him bringing down the load bearing pillars that supported the temple where his enemies were feasting. He was able to topple the structure, killing the assembled rulers of Philistia.

In the end, the name of Jehovah triumphed over false gods and Samson lived up to the name his mother had given him. He went out in a blaze of glory.

He didn't truly live up to his name until the end of his life, but in his final act he made up for lost time. He had many character fails along the way but in the end he went from Failure to Victor.

David, the Murderer

David, King of Israel, hand-picked by God, was a man after

God's own heart.[5] He started his journey in life strong. He was the brave youth who took on the Philistine hero Goliath with only courage and a sling shot. He was a psalmist, a man of character. David was man who, even though the prophet Samuel had anointed him to be king of Israel in place of King Saul, refused to resort to assassination to get to the promised throne.

But then along came the beautiful Bathsheba and everything unraveled. Lust lead to adultery and adultery led to murder in an effort to cover up what he'd done. In the end, cover ups never cover up much. Sin is always discovered and revealed. Sometimes not in our lifetime but eventually the light shines in those dark corners. David's cover up only lasted until Nathan the prophet got to him and then it was revealed and he was punished.

Have you made a choice that resulted in horrible fallout? Have the consequences led you to believe that your story is over, and God is through with you? That doesn't have to be the case.

It wasn't with David. He repented and God forgave him. He went on to write more psalms after his sin with Bathsheba, including Psalms 51, 102, 130, and 143, that have resonated with and encouraged people down through the millenia.[6]

I realize that God doesn't grade on a curve, but still, I take comfort in reading about all David's glaring sins and seeing that God forgave him. Surely, he should have racked up enough sins to forever ruin his relationship with his Creator, to leave him useless for the kingdom of God. He didn't. He continued to rule Israel and he designed the temple his son Solomon would one day build. God forgave and continued to use David in spite of the many troubles that followed him after his sins. He will forgive and continue to use me. He will forgive and continue to use you, too.

Peter the Pebble

John labels himself as the disciple Jesus loved, but I think Peter is the one most of the rest of us love. I know I do. I appreciate his enthusiasm and take comfort in his blunders as I remember how blunder prone I am. One moment Jesus is renaming him to honor a moment of great insight and the next our Lord is chastising him. Peter's foot was so often in his mouth it's a wonder he didn't chew his sandals to pieces. His life was one of spiritual highs and lows – jumping out of a boat to come to Jesus and actually walking on the water[7], cutting off a soldier's ear when Judas came to betray him[8] and then denying he even knew his master.[9] If his story had ended there it would have been tragic, indeed.

It didn't. Peter the coward, who carried the guilt of denying his beloved teacher, was given a second chance. He made the most of that chance, spreading the good news of Jesus' resurrection, boldly telling his people they needed to repent. A leader in the early church, he was imprisoned and beaten[10] but that never stopped him from telling of what he'd seen – Jesus the Christ, risen and alive. His letters to the church endure as part of our New Testament and have guided countless multitudes of believers who came after him. What a difference between that new and improved version of Peter and the old Peter who was afraid to acknowledge his friendship with Christ.

And what a difference between him and the disciple Judas, who betrayed Jesus to his enemies. Judas, like Peter, was grieved over his actions, but where Peter found forgiveness, repented and went on to do great things, Judas ended his life.[11] His story stopped after his betrayal. He stopped it by his own hand.

When we sin, when we take wrong turns on our life journey we are always faced with a decision. Will I be a Judas or a Peter? Will I give up or will I ask forgiveness and go on?

Jesus said that he would deny in heaven any man who

denied him on earth.[12] Peter did that, and yet Jesus restored him to the fold, challenged him to care for the other sheep of the flock.[13] Why?

I believe it came down to a matter of the heart. Jesus knew Peter had a repentant heart, knew Peter truly, in spite of his moment of fear and cowardice, loved his Lord. God wasn't through with Peter. That dark moment of his life wasn't the last of his story. The best, most epic part of his life was still to come. In the end, he became Peter the Rock, a man whose life was built on the Rock of Ages. Peter is proof that what God builds will outlast our mistakes.

Saul the persecutor

Here is a case where someone started out sure that he knew exactly what he was doing and what his life should look like. Saul, filled with misplaced zeal, thought he was accomplishing exactly what he had been put on earth to do. His mission was to eliminate those deluded Jews who were proclaiming they had found the Messiah. They were a blight on the people of God, and he was going to do everything in his power to remove that blight.

We first see him mentioned at the stoning of a Jesus follower named Stephen. Saul wasn't casting stones, but he was right there, watching over the perpetrators' coats.[14] The account of Stephen's stoning goes on to tell us that Saul approved of his people's vicious turning on one of their own.[15]

After this, great persecution broke out against the church at Jerusalem, and Jesus' believers were scattered. This was the beginning of Saul's first misguided crusade. We are told that "Godly men buried Stephen and mourned deeply for him. But Saul began to destroy the church. Going from house to house, he dragged off men and women and put them in prison."[16] All in the name of God, of course. Talk about making a name for itself. The very name Saul was enough to strike fear in the hearts of early believers.

As Saul journeyed to Damascus, where he planned to destroy more followers of the Way, Jesus, himself, confronted him, calling down from heaven the famous words, "Saul, Saul, why do you persecute me?"[17] Terrified, Saul fell to the ground, and when he finally arose on shaky knees, the man who thought he had such insights was blind.

God graciously returned Saul's sight to him, and you can read about that in the ninth chapter of Acts. More important than receiving back his physical sight was the healing of his spiritual blindness. Saul was a new man.

With a new name. We're not really told what the deal was with that new name. Suddenly, in Acts 13:9, we read that he was also called Paul. We can conjecture that he decided it might be best to go with a name that didn't terrify his fellow Jews. We can conjecture that someone, somewhere, dubbed him Paul. Perhaps, since the name is derived from the Latin adjective meaning small or humble,[18] he, himself, took it to symbolize the new man he had become. We don't know.

The one thing we do know is that this man was no longer the same. Under the name of Saul he had persecuted people. Under the name of Paul he became one of the persecuted and worked tirelessly to share the truth that he had discovered with others. Under the name of Paul he, himself suffered greatly and considered it an honor to suffer for Christ. Under the name of Paul he became the greatest missionary Christendom has ever known.

Can you envision someone saying to him, "Wait a minute. Aren't you Saul, the man who persecuted all who follow Christ?"

Maybe he would reply, "I was that man, but now I'm in Christ and I am a new creation. I was once arrogant and vicious. God has humbled me and filled me with His love. Please, call me Paul."

WHAT WRONG TURNS have you taken? Did you lose sight of God's goodness like Naomi and give up on life? Have you failed to appreciate your gift like Samson, done things you're ashamed of like Moses and David? Have you made blunders like Saul? Have you stalled out somewhere along the way? What steps of faith were you too afraid to take?

Addressing those questions will have value only if you use them to point you to God and allow Him to turn you in a new direction. Here in the present the question isn't so much "Where have I been? but "What have I learned from that and where do I go from here?"

I love the message in Ephesians 2:10. "For we are God's workmanship, created in Christ Jesus to do good works, which God prepared in advance for us to do."[19] God has called us all to serve Him in some way. He has good works planned for us, has a job set aside for each of us. God created us humans to reflect His glory and goodness That purpose doesn't change simply because we get sidetracked.

Divorce, adultery, theft, money mismanagement, bad parenting, grudges and estrangement from loved ones or friends – sadly, these things happen even among believers. We fall prey to deception, we get angry and make rash decisions, we give in to selfishness, we wimp out when called to stand up for what is right. Rather like those people we read about in the Bible. Sometimes we let fear hold us back from taking on certain responsibilities.

When we have sinned, there is always a choice to be made. Do we acknowledge when we've done something wrong and ask for forgiveness or do we justify our actions? Do we look at the mess we've fallen into and give up and stay there or do we go on? Do we look to God for help, or do we look to blame Him? Do we step out in faith and do what we've been called to do or do we shrink back?

If you are living with the fallout of wrong choices that has blinded you to God's call on your life, may I suggest some steps for you to take?

1. Acknowledge your wrongdoing and ask for forgiveness, first from God and then from the people you've wronged.

You can't fix something that is broken unless you first admit that it's broken. When we ask for forgiveness, we are acknowledging, not only our wrongdoing, but the fact that we offended God and have hurt others in the process.

1. Search for a Scripture you can claim and cling to that will remind you that you are on a new road.

There is nothing Satan likes better than to discourage us from moving forward. He will do that by trying to keep us looking backward at things we've done wrong and telling us we are not worthy of God's redemption and calling on our lives. He will tell us we're incapable of doing what we were called to do. He will do his best to cripple us – physically, emotionally, spiritually – in order to stop our story and keep us from the journey God has set before us. He'll tell us it's too late to start again. Or he'll tell us we are not qualified to do anything worthwhile. But that is just plain wrong so don't give him that power.

We can all claim the message in Ephesians 2:10. God has prepared good works for all of us. There is no time limit or expiration date anywhere in that verse. No matter what you've done or failed to do, no matter whether you've stumbled or failed to even get started, your story isn't over.

1. Redirect your focus.

There comes a point, whether it's after a physical injury or some kind of loss, that you have to start looking forward and making plans for how your life will be from now on. It is the same when we've taken a spiritual nosedive. Like Moses, you may have been experiencing a time in the wilderness but now God is calling you out. Take time to pray and ask Him to guide you.

Keep the apostle Paul's experience in mind. After his encounter with God and his resulting blindness, he didn't go rushing off immediately, looking for something to do. He regrouped, spent time with the disciples, found his spiritual feet.[20] We, too, need to give God time to work in our hearts and minds and give us clarity of vision. We do that by following the example of the disciples and the new and forgiven Paul, who spent time seeking God's guidance before launching into the mission He had planned for them.[21]

So, how to get there?

1. Seek Wisdom

Study your Bible. (You might want to start with a word study, picking a word that describes your feelings or current need, then seeing where the word appears in Scripture and how those passages are speaking to you.) As inspiration comes to you, make note of the knowledge you're gleaning and any changes you need to make. There are always changes to make, both in our attitudes (the first change) and in our behavior.

1. Make the changes necessary for the next phase of your life.

Here's where it can get hard. Those changes God prompts us to make can look scary and they can be uncomfortable. God may ask you to give up something you've been holding tightly, something you desperately want, but something that is, ultimately, harmful to you. The changes He requires are necessary if we're going to grow into the people He wants us to be.

Change requires work. Whether we've made a mess of things, or someone has come along and torn down something good in our lives, either way we have to rebuild.

If you've lost a job, you may have to retrain for a new career. If you lost a mate you've had to rebuild your life for one instead of two. If you're ever had surgery or a serious injury, I'm sure you have come to understand in a real way how difficult and painful rebuilding can be. You probably went to physical therapy where you worked on strengthening muscles and getting back lost range of motion and motor skills. Injuring ourselves spiritually requires repair and rebuilding, too. Perhaps you've been hurt and need to allow God to heal those wounds. Perhaps you've lost confidence in your ability to use the gift God has given you. Or perhaps you're convinced that you can't rise from the rubble your life has become. Don't give up.

We work toward becoming the people God wants us to be one step at a time. One day without a drink, one apology to someone we've hurt, one first payment on a loan we neglected to repay, a refusal to go to a party where we know things will get out of hand, one Sunday walking into church after a long absence, memorizing one Bible verse.

If you've managed to change one thing, then you can continue to build on it. Another day without a drink, another determination to forgive that person who hurt you. Another day to open your Bible before heading out the door to work. Another day to find the strength to say no to old friends who want you to slip back into bad habits. Perhaps your one step involves going back to school or job training, volunteering at church. With each step we take one step in the right direction we draw closer to God, and He makes us stronger.

1. Get Support

Look for people who are strong in the faith and are living godly, wise lives, people who will be willing to mentor and encourage you as you rebuild. Join a small group or Bible study. This really isn't optional. We all need support and we all need guidance. The disciples followed Jesus and listened to his teaching. Paul spent time with the disciples before beginning his ministry. Surely none of us have our lives together more than they did.

1. Take Note

Observe what God is doing in your life. I would encourage you to write down the attitude changes and signs you see pointing you in a new and better direction. Writing about these will keep you focused and reading about them as you continue in your new direction will encourage you to stay the course.

1. Do the deeds of the New You

Tell people what God is doing in your life. Look for opportunities to help others. This may involve opening your home for a Bible study or helping at your local food bank. God may ask you to give money to a certain worthy cause or assist someone in need. He will definitely call you to spend time with Him. As you build spiritual muscle God will expect you to use it.

1. Remember

You, daughter of God, are here for a purpose. God knows you by name and is calling you to serve Him. Don't let your circumstances or past mistakes lead you to believe that you are of no use to Him. When we submit to God, in the end it is His name for us and His purpose for our lives that will stand. Remind yourself of that. Recount to yourself how He has called you and how He has worked in your life.

God is not through with you. Don't be discouraged if setbacks occur. They do for all of us. But that doesn't change the fact that we are His until our last breath. And even with that last breath we can ask forgiveness and glorify Him.

At some point we all must be reborn. We all must start again. New life, new name, new you.

God knows how to write a meaningful life story for each one of us. All we have to do to is follow His outline. Get back in the story!

1. Background information on this book was gleaned from *https://www.biblica.com/resources/scholar-notes/niv-study-bible/intro-to-isaiah/*
2. *Unexpected Journey*, Sheila Roberts, Roberts Ink,
3. Acts 7:30
4. Exodus 3:11, New International Version
5. I Samuel 13:14
6. For commentary on these Psalms, visit *https://www.bibletrack.org*
7. Matthew 14:22-29

8. John 18:10
9. Matthew 26:69-75
10. Acts 5:40; 12:2-5
11. Matthew 27:1-5
12. Matthew 10:33
13. John 21:15-17
14. Acts 7:58
15. Acts 8:1
16. Acts 8: 2,3, New International Version
17. Acts 9:4, New International Version
18. *https://www.behindthename.com/name/paul*
19. New International Version
20. Acts 9:19
21. Acts 1:12-15

SEVEN
I'M GOING TO CALL YOU ...

We've seen how important names are, seen how they impart meaning. In a perfect world, no one would hurl unwanted ones at us in anger or slap them on us behind our backs. We'd all like the names we were given at birth and the only name calling we'd hear on the block growing up would be, "Beautiful," "Cool Kid," or "Loveable

But it's not a perfect world. Children can be cruel. Adults get angry and reach for hurtful words. I think we women are especially good at wielding our words like swords. (Maybe it's because we use so many more per day than men to begin with and our verbal skills are well honed.)

It's scary how we tend to live up to our names. Consider a man mentioned briefly in the Bible named Nabal. You can find his story in the book of 1 Samuel, chapter 25. Nabal was successful. But he was also unkind and stingy, too stingy to help an up-and-coming man named David, a man who would become king of Israel. His refusal to help David and his troops was not a wise move, and it angered David so much that he was ready to attack the household of Nabal. It took the intervention of Nabal's wife, Abigail, to save the family.

Verse 25 completes the picture of Nabal. His wife tells a furious David, "...He is just like his name – his name is Fool, and folly goes with him."[1]

Every time I read about this man, I wonder what made his parents decide to give him such an unflattering name. Who would name their child Fool? Was that his original name or did his childhood behavior inspire them to give him that nickname?

Think of the nicknames children sometimes get saddled with, such as Fatso or Stinker or Troublemaker. Does the child with weight issues who is continually teased about her appearance give up and figure she is and always will be fat? Does that child then turn to food for comfort and the nickname becomes a self-fulfilling prophecy, leaving the child facing both health and self-esteem issues down the road? Does the child who's labeled a troublemaker conclude that negative attention is better than no attention and take a perverse pride in causing trouble?

We often project our unhappiness onto our children and leave them with labels that will ultimately hurt them. A great example from the Bible is Rachel, the wife of Jacob, one of the patriarchs of the Jewish faith.

You've probably read about or heard of Rachel and her sister Leah. To say these sisters weren't close would be a gross understatement. Rachel was the pretty one. Leah was ... the other sister, the less than perfect one, the girl who got overlooked.

Lo and behold, a handsome relative named Jacob arrived on the scene and fell madly in love with beautiful Rachel. Laban, the girls' daddy, knew he'd have no problem marrying off Rachel, but what to do about Leah? She was the oldest of the two and the locals weren't exactly beating a path to the tent door to ask for her hand in marriage.

Laban came up with a plan. A little trickery, a little bamboozling and Leah became the first Mrs. Jacob, which left Rachel out in the cold.

I can only imagine the scene when Rachel got wind of this. How hard for the spoiled, pretty girl!

Jacob made a deal with his father-in-law, promising to work for him for seven years and finally was allowed to marry his dream girl, making her the second Mrs. Jacob. This actually made his life more of a nightmare because now he had two women playing a game of one-ups-man-ship and using him as the pawn. Leah may not have been the prettiest sister, but she was the most fertile, having son after son, while her sister struggled with infertility.

Rachel did finally have the son she so desperately wanted, a boy who grew up to become the famous Joseph of the many-colored coat. That barely got her in the competition though, and she wasn't content.

She had one more son after Joseph, but this baby cost Rachel her life. With her last breath she named the baby Benoni, which means Son of my sorrow. (Thankfully, the baby's father changed the name to Benjamin, which means Son of My Right Hand)."[2]

Rachel's name for her baby sounds pretty much like *I wish I'd never had you* to me. Reading her story, I see a woman who'd always been spoiled, who pretty much thought about no one but herself. Even at the end of her life, instead of thinking of her baby, she could only focus on her own misery. What a blessing for the child that his father re-named him.

Is there some Rachel in all of us? Do we often project our unhappiness on others? Instead of acknowledging the decisions we made that brought us to where we are in life, it can be easier to look for someone else to blame. That someone can be a child, a spouse, a parent, a friend. The disappointment or anger bubbles to the surface and suddenly we're attaching names to people that we hope will make them as miserable as we are.

Sadly, in a moment of anger, frustration or, simply not thinking we slap negative names on our children. Have you ever called your child Stupid? Lazy? Bad? This kind of shame naming is not the way to inspire or motivate. It's certainly not the way to make our children feel secure in our love.

I confess I have certainly said some dumb things as a mother, and when I think of them, I wish I could go back in time and cover my mouth with duct tape. I finally wised up and, in recent years have worked hard to build up rather than tear down, being sure to compliment my children and grand-children on the good things I see in them. Not that I'm afraid to speak truth when it's needed (to which my longsuffering grown children will attest), but that, I now realize, has to be done in love and balanced with encouragement. (Hey, kids, I'm trying!)

Even when we don't use names, what we say to others still bestows names, either for better or for worse. According to my friend Marva Jones, who is an early childhood educator, without even saying that bad name we can wind up labelling our children.

Think of the mother, who in anger, tells her child, "I wish I'd never had you." This sentence pins a new name on a child: Unwanted. The child will bury that name and all the nega-tivity that goes along with it soul deep, and, if no one inter-venes, carry it for a lifetime and act accordingly. Imagine the insecurity and recklessness that grow out of feeling unwanted. (Perhaps you have felt unwanted by a parent and know exactly what that translates into.)

If you're helping your child with homework and you say, "I don't understand why you can't get this," your child may be hearing, "You are so stupid." If a child hears that sort of thing often enough the child will adopt a new name: Dummy or Stupid.

If your child has gained weight thanks to too many goodies or an inactive lifestyle, rather than talking about putting the child on a diet or shaming the child for craving treats, your child will be better served by a subtle shift in lifestyle: less goodies in the house, more exercise as a family, introducing nutritious snacks and slowly weeding out the junk food. How about instead of saying, "You are putting on too much weight," or "You're fat," (something the child has probably already figured out) saying things like, "Let's work on getting healthier." Monitoring our words and keeping the focus away from that whole area of appearance allows the child to develop new habits and gain confidence.

I don't subscribe to the school of thought that believes competition is a bad thing, and I don't think every child should get a ribbon at the track meet. Success and hard work should be rewarded, and failure should be admitted. We all fail once in a while, and failure can be a valuable learning tool. We assess what we did wrong and try again. We learn the value of practice and persistence. We can even learn that what we're trying maybe isn't for us after all and that we need to assess our talents, potential, and skills, and pursue different interests. But this can be a painful process and it's important to handle our children's failures in such a way as to keep them moving forward in life. I do believe that every child should be comforted and encouraged when failure rears its ugly head.

Comments like, "We're proud of how hard you tried," may not erase the disappointment of striking out but they will ease the sting. Allowing a child to fail is okay. Being critical and rubbing in the failure is not.

Questions like, "Do you think you could have done better?"

and "How do you think you can improve?" when a child has gotten a bad grade acknowledge the problem but don't condemn. Also, praising any success or improvement is always an excellent way to start a conversation with a child about scholastic achievement. I've known parents who were never satisfied with their children's progress in school. A report card filled with B's would, instead of compliments, receive comments such as, "If you can get B's, you can get A's." Maybe this is true. But maybe it's not. Perhaps that child worked very hard to get a B. Or a C. Never acknowledging the amount of work a child has done or the level of achievement that child has reached sends the underlying message that nope, Junior still hasn't measured up. Junior then adopts the name Failure.

Instead of starting with that "That's not good enough," we can say, "I appreciate how hard you worked," and celebrate the moment of success or offer comfort and encouragement. There will be time after that to ask, "Do you think you can top that next time?"

Words aren't the only way we slap labels on our children. I think back to my childhood struggles with math and can still picture my father, who was not the soul of patience, trying to help me with math problems. I can see him pulling at his hair in frustration (which was not easy to do since he had a crew cut). His body language alone was enough to make every synapse in my brain freeze. Then, of course, he'd add a few words, like, "Why can't you get this?" Finally, he'd holler, "Sam, come help your sister!"

My big brother Sam was several years older than me and a math whiz. He actually wound up teaching high school math and three generations of kids have called his phone number, which was dubbed the math hotline, for help. He would sit down and take a stab at trying to walk me through the mystery of numbers. Not an easy thing to do considering my brain was wired for creative pursuits, plus it was still frozen solid.

I wasn't a stupid child, and, for the most part, my parents applauded my accomplishments and encouraged me to develop my talents. But with mathematics, my Achilles heel, it was a different story, and it didn't take me long to conclude that, when it came to math, I was hopeless. I became Caroline Can't Do and lived up to the name, struggling my way through school math classes. I still remember jokingly asking my high school algebra teacher if I could bribe him to pass me. And we won't talk about flunking the midterm in my college math class. Beginner (also referred to as Bonehead) Algebra. (Yes, that again!)

On and on it went. Hopeless. Unteachable. That was me, I'd learned this way back in grade school. I balanced my first checking account in college by closing the account.

Early in my marriage, I tried to rise above my Caroline Can't Do name, attempting to take a more active role in our finances and master the art of balancing the checkbook. (Obviously, back in the days before you could simply hop online and check your balance.) That went well. Not.

My first solo flight with the checkbook, I announced to my husband that we were a thousand dollars in the hole. I still remember the shocked expression on his face. It turned out that we weren't. It was a case of operator error – what a relief! But that was the last time I got involved in handling the family finances.

Again, the message from this experience was clear. I just couldn't get this math stuff. Obviously, I never would. Dummy me!

Every time I was faced with anything that carried math overtones a part of me would pipe up and say, "We don't do that." And I'd agree. "Yes, you're right. We don't," and I'd shy away.

As an adult I counted on my fingers for years. It wasn't until I had children of my own and had to help them with their schoolwork that I finally began to memorize addition and subtraction facts. To this day I sometimes revert to that old habit of finger counting.

Finally, in my early fifties I decided I'd had enough of being so math challenged. I formed a club with some other women, and we started reading books on finance. We asked a local stockbroker to come and talk to us about the stock market and investing.

Then came the day when I was reading a Suze Orman book and saw a chart showing how compound interest worked. A light bulb went off and I got it. I finally understood a math concept which had seemed hopelessly complicated and which I'd never before been able to understand. Wow! Maybe I wasn't a Caroline Can't Do after all.

A great little story, isn't it? But look how long it took me to get to the point in life where I figured I could actually learn this stuff. And I do believe it all started way back with my father's frustration.

What can we do when we're trying to help our children learn something and they're not getting it? Let me suggest that we try to watch our language, both verbal and body. Not all of us are gifted teachers so if one of our children is struggling, he or she might need help from someone who speaks the child's language. It might mean finding ways to get extra time after school with the teacher, hiring a tutor, or enlisting help from a sympathetic relative.

Or a friend. When our daughter was in high school, she had trouble grasping some math concepts. One of my friends at church was able to help her. "I get the way she explains it," my daughter said. Once we found someone who could communicate well on this subject with her, she was good to go.

We all have areas where we shine and ones where we struggle. So do our children. I think it's all right to say, "This isn't your forte," to a child as long as we add, "But that's okay because you have other God-given talents." (And be aware of those talents, so when you child asks you what they are you can name them!)

With schoolwork, there isn't always the option to move on to something else. That English or science class must be passed, and those algebra problems need to get solved. Let's encourage our children to do their best but not berate them when they don't excel and let's try to find them the help they need. Grades should be recognized as tools for assessing progress rather than worth.

Let's apply that same principle to ourselves. Our failures or lack of skill in certain areas don't make us less loved by God or less valuable as a person, so let's not let them induce us to shame name ourselves.

Another action that speaks loudly is withholding evidence of love when you're angry. That says loud and clear, "You're not good enough," and bestows the name Unloved.

My husband once shared that his mom, when displeased with him, would give him the silent treatment. Finally, his father would have to step in and say, "You'd better go apologize to your mother."

I know for a fact that my mother-in-law loved her son and was proud of him, especially of his accomplishments as an adult. She was a fabulous mother-in-law and I adored her. Sadly, though, my husband never felt close to her. In spite of the fact that she loved him, her treatment of him as a child when he misbehaved told him something very different and prevented them from ever becoming close.

There's really no such thing as "I'm not speaking to you," because our behavior speaks volumes.

There is, however, a difference between, "I'm not speaking to you," and "You need to go to your room and think about your behavior." Sometimes, separating ourselves from our offspring so we can each have a cooling off period can be a good idea. (I know I should have done this more!) It gives children a chance to consider their actions and parents time to think about what they want to discuss and what is the most appropriate discipline.

And discipline does need to be meted out. Otherwise, if we don't, we can send the message to our children that we don't care enough to bother with them. Once more, that brings with it the name Unloved.

It can also bring another name: Center of the Universe. I think of King David and his son Absalom. Absalom of the beautiful long hair. Absalom the conspirator, who went after his father's throne. That Absalom. If you're unfamiliar with this man or you want a refresher course on him you can read his story in 2 Samuel, chapters thirteen through eighteen.

One of the most telling pieces of Scripture regarding David's parenting and how Absalom turned out can actually be found in 1 Kings 1:6: "His father [David] had never rebuked him at any time by asking, "Why have you done this?..."[3] Daddy could never bring himself to correct his son's behavior, thus unwittingly naming his son Perfect.

When you're perfect, well, you're perfect. You can do no wrong. This was how Absalom saw himself. He was always justified in everything he did. Sadly, everything he did wasn't justifiable.

While we don't want to negatively label our children, we also don't want them to become self-centered and undisciplined. We don't want them to attach the name Center of the

Universe to themselves. I suspect we can all think of children (and adults) who have claimed this name for themselves. And that, is the other end of the spectrum of negative names. The person living up to that name cares little for others and certainly struggles with the concept of submitting to the will of God and serving Christ.

Discipline and punishment are necessary, even though most of us don't often enjoy meting them out. There is truth in that old parental saying, "This hurts me more than it does you." But whatever the punishment, we want to make clear that it is for correcting behavior that's bad and unacceptable in a child of a God-fearing family. Reminding our children that they are special to God, that God wants the best for them and wants them to grow up to live lives that will both honor Him and bring them contentment is vital. It addresses the behavior but doesn't label the child. This way the child always carries the name Loved.

When we know we're loved, we feel confident to grow and try new things. When we don't, it makes us tentative, fearful. With children it doesn't take much to embed a lack of confidence. Again, our words have such power. Even when we think of them as harmless. Which brings us to the subject of teasing. While appearing to be fun and good-natured, this can cause hurt and slap unwanted labels on a child.

One of my brothers once gave me this definition of teasing. It is joking about something that is the opposite of what's really true. Jokingly saying, "It's a pity she's not pretty," when your niece has just won a beauty contest is something the beauty queen is going to accept. Say that when she's an insecure teen and, as happened with me, you may see very different results. Saying your son is king of the bathroom because he spends so much time in the shower or fussing with his appearance is one thing. Saying it when the child has a problem with bed wetting is quite another. That's an extreme example, but I'm sure you get the idea. Anything that humiliates or challenges the intrinsic worth a child produces no good results.

Negative teasing is another way we slap discouraging names on people. Comments like, "Way to go, Klutz," or "Leave it to Suzi to screw it up," can get internalized easily and quickly. Teasing about first attempts at a skill that don't go well, or sarcastic comments such as, "Good one," when a child (or adult) makes a mistake can humiliate and discourage. We don't have to hand out too many of them to convince that person to give up and not pursue an interest long enough to master it. Hand out enough snide remarks and teasing and even a strong person will become discouraged. Do this to a child and that child will self-label as Not Good Enough.

I've seen proof of that in the stories so many women have shared with me. Teasing often has its roots in anger, disappointment, jealousy or insecurity. You may have encountered this in your own life with someone attempting to build herself up by tearing you down. Or perhaps you had a parent who was insecure in his or her own gifts and expected you to make up the difference in what that parent was lacking. Pride was at stake and when you didn't live up to the parent's expectations you were put down or ridiculed.

There's a difference between laughing at a silly situation and laughing at the person. We can laugh at ourselves over silly mistakes because we are all human.

One of my embarrassing stories involved tripping over a practice balance beam when leading a group of kindergarten gymnastics students around the gym floor in a warm-up game of Follow the Leader. Thankfully, they didn't follow me in that move. I did a face plant in front of, not only the kids I was teaching, but their parents as well, who were watching from the sidelines. Talk about embarrassing. But I could laugh at myself because no one was hurt. All my body parts normally work fine (when I'm paying attention), so no harm, no foul. But what if I was a child in a competition and something like that happened? Then it wouldn't be so funny.

Laughing at yourself is one thing. Laughing at others is quite another. Our children will be teased enough by other children, especially if they have a learning disability or speech impediment or physical flaw. Home should be a safety zone where the child is free from that sort of thing. Which means sibling teasing and put-downs are not allowed. There will be enough people to come along and label our children with negative names. We don't need to add to the load.

The same thing applies to adults. Aging doesn't make us immune from hurt or embarrassment. How do you speak about those close to you, both when you're with them and when you're not?

The way we speak about our spouses when we're irritated often paints an inaccurate picture of them for others. When we complain that, "My husband is a tightwad," or "He's such a slob," we are painting a one-dimensional picture of that person. If a man jokingly says, "My wife is an airhead," what mental image comes to mind? Surely the wife isn't an airhead all the time, otherwise how stupid does that make the man for marrying her? Yet, we often hear people assigned these kinds of names and we do form a certain mental image.

When I was young wife and not so wise, I used to complain to a friend who didn't know my husband well about all the things he wasn't doing right. One day she said something unflattering about him and I became highly offended. How dare she say such a thing about my man?

"Sheila, I'm only going by what you've told me," she replied in her own defense.

Ouch! I realized she was right. My complaining didn't give

an accurate description of my husband because it left out all his good characteristics. I changed my wicked ways in a hurry.

We all like to vent when we feel we've been wronged. After a hurtful or insulting encounter with someone our first response is to call that person a name, if not to her face, then for sure behind her back. Ever hear someone say any of the following? "He's a jerk," or "She's a bitch," or "That woman is poison."

Some people live up to those names, and I can understand the desire, after being burned, to point to the fire. But while it feels good to vent and tell *someone* just how bad that person is and how wrongly the person treated us, talking negatively about others when we're angry paints a one-sided picture and slaps a negative name on that person.

Gossip also paints a one-sided picture. When we blab about others' missteps, we are slapping labels on them and giving them a name that precedes them.

Recently, a friend shared information about someone who was just beginning to attend our church, information that I didn't need, that was none of my business. Looking back, I realize I should have recognized the gossip for what it was and immediately turned the conversation. Since I didn't, by the time I met this person I was already prejudiced and had bestowed the name Trouble on the newcomer. What I heard led to an impression, that impression led to a name, and the name left me leery of having much contact with the person. It took a while for me to see there was more to my new acquaintance than a past mistake.

This experience was a good reminder that every story has two sides, and I shouldn't pre-judge people's every word and action according to gossip I have heard. It's also been a huge reminder to me to not only watch what comes out of my mouth but to also watch what I let go in my ears.

One of my husband's favorite sayings when someone misbehaves is, "He's got issues."

How true! We all have issues. We're all dealing with sin and bad habits and bad attitudes. So maybe we should cut each other some slack. That jerk who said something mean may simply be having a bad day or have had one too many drinks. (And we all know that alcohol doesn't always bring out the best in people.) That so-called bitch may be experiencing PMS. (Something that often turned me into a raging monster!) Or she may be lacking in social skills and not understand how to use diplomacy when dealing with others. Okay, and yes, he may be a jerk and she may be a stinker, but if that's the case the person is quite capable of revealing his or her faults without anyone broadcasting them.

The Bible tells us to "pray for those who despitefully use us."[4] And for good reason. Often, that person who lashes out at us or treats us unfairly is suffering, struggling to realize who she or he was meant to be. We are called to be patient with one another. There's a reason Mom always said, "If you can't say anything nice don't say anything at all."

Mom is backed up by the apostle James, who said, "The tongue also is a fire, a world of evil among the parts of the body. It corrupts the whole person, sets the whole course of his life on fire, and is itself set on fire by hell."[5] Yikes! Pretty strong language. But think of the consequences of our hateful words.

I'm writing this book during a time of racial tension here in the U.S. We've seen protests and riots. Many of my black friends have remembered, and not with fondness, times when people hurled racial slurs at them. These are born of hatred and fear, and they spawn more of the same. Names hurt and divide

If you doubt that think of the names thrown around during World War II. Jap was not a friendly nickname. Neither was Kraut. During other times in history we see nicknames given to ethnic groups, names meant to hurt and belittle. The Chinese were called Chinks, the Irish Micks. On and on it goes. Disparaging names not only hurt and divide, but they also inflame and incite.

Even within the body of Christ we like to label each other – the frozen chosen, holy rollers. Haha. But is God laughing? I wonder. Again, these names that might seem funny only serve to insult other believers who love God. They allow us to position ourselves as superior to others and that is not something that will bring unity.

James goes on to say, "With the tongue we praise our Lord and Father, and with it we curse men, who have been made in God's likeness. Out of the same mouth come praise and cursing. My brothers, this should not be."[6]

No, it shouldn't, but it often is. What's the cure for this kind of behavior? We can start with an attitude of humility. Not one of us is perfect so not one of us has the right to look down on another.

When someone has hurt us our first response is often to complain to our spouse or go to phone and text our best friend about the offender or get on social media with finger pointing. But really, the one we need to tell is our heavenly Father. Our first response should be to ask God for His wisdom and the strength to forgive.

Sometimes, repairing a breech in a relationship is as simple as saying, "That hurt me." People often lash out not realizing how deeply their words have cut us. A simple dialogue framed in humility to point out the problem can end it thus killing that embryo grudge in us before it has time to grow into a monster.

When we have a problem with someone it should be handled in a Biblical manner. If you can't work things out one on one, try again, this time with someone who can, hopefully, negotiate peace between the two of you.[7] This will go much farther toward fixing a problem than complaining behind the person's back and slapping a negative label on that person.

What do we teach our children when we call other people names? Nothing good. Let's instead teach them by example to apply the Golden Rule when speaking to each other. "In everything do to others as you would have them do to you."[8] Let's remind ourselves of that rule when we're tempted to let our tongues catch fire.

On the other hand, think of how we can bless others by words of kindness and encouragement. Think of how inspiring positive names are.

Here's a great example of how a positive name can take the sting from negative circumstances and become a vote of confidence. One of my readers shared that her mother named her Joy. She wasn't named under the best of circumstances because the father had left for Florida with another woman. Mama had a different name picked out originally, but when she looked at her baby daughter she thought, *This is my life, my joy*, and she named her girl accordingly. A negative got turned into a positive. A woman who could have become bitter and resentful and taken her disappointment out on her child chose to see beyond her hurt. A sad story was given a happy ending and Joy's name became a testimony to the fact that good can come out of bad.

One of my sisters-in-law has a cousin called Happy. His parents were older when Mom became pregnant with him and she thought she had a malignant tumor. They were so pleased to learn that tumor was really a baby that, instead of the name they'd picked they wound up calling the boy Happy. This man lives up to his name. I've never seen him without a smile on his face.

Speaking of smiles, my brother Sam, the math genius, received a great nickname when he was teaching: Smilin' Sam. Smilin' Sam has been and always is the life of the party.

What godly character do you see God building in your child? Point it out. What good things do you see in your spouse? In your siblings? In your friends? When was the last time you pinned an encouraging name on someone? It's not too late to start now.

And it's not too late to apologize for wrong and hurtful things you've said. Sadly, we can never go back in time and swallow those harsh words or undo unkind behavior. We can, however, move forward and be aware of what we are telling others, both with our words and our actions.

There is always a choice. We can exercise our mouths for good or for bad. We can forgive and show kindness, or we can get even and wound. We can put down or we can build up. Let's not use our bodies as an instrument of hurt. Let's use them as a tool to build up each other.

Here is the is good advice from the apostle Paul for all of us who go by the name of Christian: "Get rid of all bitterness, rage, anger, harsh words and slander, as well as all types of evil behavior. Instead, be kind to each other, tenderhearted, forgiving one another just as God through Christ has forgiven you."[9]

When we interact with each other let's be mindful of what names we're doling out and what self-image we are building in those around us. We want to build up the body of Christ, not tear it down.

Let's also remember to be mindful of what we say to ourselves. Have you been disgusted with something you did and called yourself a name?

My husband pointed out to me that I'm often guilty of that. I'll get frustrated and mutter something like, "Sheila, you dope." Or I'll use other favorite words such as Dummy and Turkey.

The problem with this is twofold. First, when we call

ourselves names, we paint a negative picture of ourselves and give others permission to see us in that same light and treat us accordingly. Secondly, and even more important, when we insult ourselves, we also insult the One who made us. Yes, we all do dumb things but that doesn't mean we're stupid.

I think of a line from a children's song that I was taught in Sunday School. "Oh, be careful little mouth, what you say." The reason for that, as the song goes on to explain is that the Father is looking down on us.

Our heavenly Father is watching. Let's honor Him with our attitudes and our mouths. Let's be careful what names we dole out to each other.

1. New International Version

2. Genesis 35:18, Amplified Bible

3. Amplified Bible

4. Matthew 5:44, King James translation

5. James 3:6, New International Version

6. James 3:9, 10 New International Version

7. Matthew 18:15-17

8. Matthew 7:12, New Revised Standard Version

9. Ephesians 4:31, 32, New Living Translation

EIGHT
NEW BEGINNINGS, NEW NAME

I can't say this enough. It's never too late for a new name and a new start. I learned this, not only from what I've read in the Bible, but from my own life experience.

Many years ago, some of the women at my church worked through a study book titled *Experiencing God: Knowing and Doing the Will of God*, by Henry and Richard Blackaby and Claude King. Much of the material I already knew, and I can remember thinking, What is there in this for me to learn? (No conceit there!)

As it turns out, there was something very important for me to learn. The authors of this study pointed out something I had never noticed. Often, when God was about to do a work in someone's heart and life, He changed that person's name.

Abram, whose name meant Exalted Father or Father of height, ironically, had no son to help him settle the new land God had promised. But God had a plan for Abram and with that plan came a new name. He became Abraham, and this new name meant Father of a Multitude.[1] His wife, Sarai, whose name meant Princess,[2] became Sarah, a princess of a very different kind, the mother of nations. These name changes came along with a promise on God's part that Abram would, indeed, have a son. And, more than that, the one son would grow into a multitude of descendants. An entire nation would come from Abraham.

Could God have kept his promise to Abram without changing his name? Of course, He could have, but the new name served as a reminder that God was going to work in Abram's life in an amazing, new way. A new name for both himself and his wife served as a reminder of what lay ahead, proof of what was yet to come. It gave them both something to live for. So good-bye Abram and Sarai. Hello Abraham and Sarah.

Jacob, Abraham's grandson, that sneaky cheater whose name meant Supplanter, is another great example of how a new life and a new name can go hand in hand. If you're not familiar with the story of the sibling rivalry between Jacob and his older brother Esau, you can find it in Genesis 25:21-34 and Genesis 27. The world's first soap opera!

Jacob may have been a manipulator and a sneak, but I will give him credit for knowing a good thing when he saw it. We're told in Hebrews 12:15,16 that his older brother, Esau, although he had a position of honor and responsibility as the firstborn male in the family, didn't appreciate what he had. He sold his position (his birthright) to his brother simply for a good meal. It wasn't until later, when Jacob, under Mom's tutelage, tricked their father out of the blessing that was due to the oldest that Esau began to see what he'd lost. It was something Jacob had seen all along and wanted.

Things did not go well after this second stunt and Jacob was forced to flee for his life. Away from his mother and father, he learned firsthand from his crafty Uncle Laban how it felt to be tricked and swindled. Add to that a homecoming where he was unsure of his welcome and the stage was set for a spiritual encounter. He came away from that encounter with a new name: Israel.

In Genesis 32:27, 28, we see the significance of that name, given him by the mysterious "man" with whom he wrestled during that long night before meeting his brother again after many years: "Your name shall no longer be called Jacob, but Israel, for you have striven with God and with men and have prevailed."[3] Here was a name to inspire confidence, to show Jacob that he would survive meeting the brother who had once been ready to murder him as revenge for what he'd done. It showed, not only Jacob's persistence, but also served as a reminder that God was a central part of his life.

His descendants are a living testament to God's active involvement in their lives down through the centuries. God has protected His people from annihilation from the very beginning of their race. As with their forefather Jacob, they have prevailed.

I used to think God interacting with people in such an astonishing way was for those Bible heroes, not everyday people such as myself. Until I had an epiphany and a name change. And it all started with a study book I wasn't that excited to study!

I still remember the moment. I was alone in a room in the church basement that we were using for our women's Bible study, where we were working through the Blackabys' book. I was waiting for everyone else to arrive when a voice, so strong it was almost audible, spoke to me. To Sheila who had experienced her share of spiritual ups and downs and struggles. To Sheila who was constantly worried about money – a long-standing battle that had gotten worse thanks to some difficult circumstances we'd been experiencing over a span of five years.

"Enough," said the Voice. "From now on you are not going

to worry about money. You are going to trust Me to provide for you, and your new name is Sheila the Faithful."

Oh, my! Oh, my! Had this really happened to me? I was beside myself, overwhelmed at the experience I'd just had sitting in that empty classroom in the church basement. I'd had AN ENCOUNTER! With God!

Hardly able to contain myself, I shared with our pastor's wife the moment she entered the room. Happily for me, she didn't doubt my experience. She didn't question my sanity or ask me if I was sure I hadn't imagined the whole thing. Instead, she was thrilled for me, congratulated me on my new name. And from that time onward, whenever she'd see me, she'd greet me with, "Sheila the Faithful, how are you doing?"

Well, once you've opened your big mouth and shared your new name, you have to live up to it. So I began to do exactly that. Looking back, I am amazed at the change in myself. I had always fretted about financial problems, always worried about how we were going to pay for this or that. I stopped. Cold Turkey.

Soon after this experience, it came time to come up with college money we'd promised our son when he switched from a two-year junior college to a four-year out-of-state college. My husband wondered aloud where we were going to get it.

I said, "I don't know, but God is going to provide it."

And He did. In all kinds of ways, from a small inheritance to all manner of part-time jobs for me. The money came in as we needed it. The money has come in as we've needed it ever since.

All right! Hurdle jumped. Success.

Then came the day when the Voice spoke again, this time not so dramatically but in a whisper. "New testing is going to come in the area of your health."

A year later it did, when I discovered I had uterine cancer.

Here was yet another opportunity to trust God and to keep walking the walk with Him even though I was going through the Valley of the Shadow of Death.

Other tests and losses have come since, but God remains my rock.

That first encounter and new name was a life changer for me. I took it to heart, in much the same way as I so long ago took that negative name, Ugly Duckling to heart. Only this time, with positive results. I internalized God's name for me. I allowed it to change my attitude and reshape my life. I took it seriously and began to live accordingly. And, as we are wont to do, I was alert for proofs of the dependability of God as well as noting times when I triumphed over circumstances and lived up to this name. In the same way a child will behave to live up to either a positive or negative name, every time I saw God's faithfulness it reinforced my own behavior. I wasn't blind to His working in my life and was, therefore able to point to it. That, in turn, strengthened my confidence and trust and conditioned my behavior.

I continue to remember the name He gave me. I hope I can continue to live up to it.

Why am I sharing this? To encourage you. Perhaps you've reached a point in life where it's time to shed a dark and discouraging name you've been living under. Perhaps God is wanting to do a new work in you. Perhaps He is about to give you a new name.

This is not to say that you must have a dramatic encounter with God for a change in attitude to be viable. You don't need a burning bush or to hear a voice from heaven as Saul did on the road to Damascus. God works uniquely in all of us. When He first appeared to Abram it was in a vision.[4] When Jacob had his startling wrestling match with the Angel of the LORD it was in the midst of a time of intense fear when he was alone and about to face the brother he'd wronged so many years ago.[5]

Your interaction with God will be equally unique to you and your circumstances. God may speak to your heart through a specific Scripture or bring to mind a thought as you're praying. Something in your pastor's sermon might jump out at you. Our God isn't restricted to a formula when dealing with His children. We certainly don't do that with our own offspring because we know they are all different. God understands that about us as well and deals with us accordingly.

He works in our lives when and how He sees fit, so you don't need to buy a baby name book and start reading through it for ideas or sit down with your friends and ask for suggestions. Just be open to allowing God to work in your life, to show you where your perceptions have been wrong and allow you to see yourself as He sees you. When we are in prayer, when we are reading our Bible, when we are putting ourselves at the feet of Jesus, we are making ourselves ready for whatever spiritual lessons He wants to teach us. Jeremiah 29:13 assures us that when we are seeking God with our whole heart that we will find Him.

A good verse to chew on is another verse from that same book, Jeremiah 29:11. Here we see God's words to His people: "'For I know the plans I have for you,' declares the LORD, 'plans to prosper you and not to harm you, plans to give you hope and a future.'"[6]

To whom was God speaking? He was speaking to His chosen people, the descendants of Abraham, the nation of Israel, a people in exile. All was not well with them when Jeremiah shared these words, but God spoke to them anyway, because God could see ahead to the good things He had planned.

Surely it's the same with us. We see our failures, God sees

how He can use us. We see where we've stumbled, He sees how, once we reach out to Him, He will pull us back up. We see our unworthiness. He makes us worthy. We get distracted and stalled, sure we have nowhere to go from here, He sees where He wants to take us.

Peter considered himself as a deserter, a man no longer worthy of Jesus' affection. *May as well go back to fishing.* Which was exactly what he was doing when Jesus had that famous post-resurrection talk with him. Where Peter saw himself as a failure, Jesus saw him as a fisher of men and leader, asking Peter to shepherd His flock of new believers.[7]

Our perceptions of who we are tend to get all tangled up in our circumstances or what others tell us we should believe about ourselves (which may or may not be accurate). As with labeling and name-calling, we see one small facet of ourselves and call it the whole. God sees the whole and polishes us one facet at a time.

Know that as God changes your heart. He will also help you to change your behavior and your life. Old labels do not have to stick. When we as parents name our children, we envision good things for them. It is even more so with our heavenly Father. He has the perfect name in mind for you and He wants to see you enjoy the spiritual blessings and contentment that come from living up to that name.

So, what can we do to get that new name? Nothing in and of ourselves. We need to simply be open to the voice of God.

If you're like me, you appreciate specific suggestions and practical how-to's and not vague generalizations. This is the closest I can come to giving you some suggestions on finding and growing into a new name and a new you.

Pray, and ask God:

- Is there a name I've carried around that has hindered my spiritual growth or robbed me of joy? (If you don't already know it, He will bring it to mind.)
- Have I let others attach negative names to me?
- Has my behavior earned me a negative name? If so, what steps should I take to change that?
- Do You have a better name in mind for me?

Every day, as you study your Bible, ask yourself:

- Is there a message in this passage of Scripture for me?
- How can I apply what I'm reading to my own life?

Then...

Come full circle back to prayer. Thank God for His love and forgiveness. Tell Him that you are willing to submit to His will for your life.

Use the story of the Old Testament prophet Samuel as your inspiration. Remember Samuel? His mother dedicated him to serve God and, once he was old enough, she brought him to the Temple.

You can read about his nighttime encounter with God in I Samuel 3. God called his name in the middle of the night. He went to Eli the priest, under whom he served, sure Eli had called him. "Nope, wasn't me," said Eli. (Sheila paraphrase here.) He sent the boy back to bed and again God called him. After Samuel appeared at Eli's bedside a third time, the old priest figured out what was going on. His advice to Samuel is good advice for all of us: "... if he calls you say, 'Speak, LORD, for your servant is listening.'"[8]

As you listen with a servant's heart, I am convinced that the

Holy Spirit will work in your life, and you'll begin to see where He wants to change you. As your eyes are opened, you'll be able to shed that negative label. And yes, you may very likely come away with a different name than the negative one you've carried and a whole new attitude toward life.

Speaking of new, remember "... anyone who belongs to Christ has become a new person. The old life is gone; a new life has begun!"⁹

Think of the delight that comes with the word new. New house, new car, new hairstyle, new job, new baby, new boyfriend, new beginning. When we hear that word, we think shiny, pretty, exciting, promising, adventure, fresh starts. That's the word that applies to us as believers when God goes to work. The old is gone. If you have taken Christ as your Lord and Savior, you are already a new person. All that is left is to allow God to transform you.

So, congratulations on the new and improving you. Congratulations that the old is gone. God has plans for you.

1. Many websites discuss this. Here is one: https://lifehopeandtruth.com/bible/blog/abram-renamed-abraham/
2. https://www.biblegateway.com/resources/all-women-bible/Sarah-Sarai-Sara
3. New International Version
4. Genesis 15:1
5. Genesis 32:22-24
6. New International Version
7. Matthew 4:18-20; John 21:15-17
8. I Samuel 3:9, New International Version
9. 2 Corinthians 5:17 New Living Translation

NINE
NEW NAME = NEW LIFE

I still remember the day our second daughter officially became ours. She was a cute, little bug, all of four years old when we all left the courthouse together after the judge officially proclaimed us parents and child.

"Now we can live happily ever after," she said. Talk about adorable overload.

But having a new surname doesn't mean you instantly know how to live in the family that carries that name. It took a while for certain realities to sink in, the first one being that our little girl was now with us until she grew up and she didn't get to move on to a new home where the proverbial grass looked greener. This was a permanent deal. We were family. She also had to learn that there were rules for every member of our family, including her.

We loved this little girl like crazy (still do), and because of that love we wanted to everything in our power to mold her character and set her up for a good life. This involved discipline. Unlike God's, our discipline wasn't perfect, but she had to suffer through it, anyway.

Sometimes she didn't particularly want to suffer through that discipline, and as she got older, she and I had some exciting, hormonally driven screaming matches. (Her: "I do not have PMS!" Me: "Me, either!")

We loved our girl too much not to correct her when she needed it. We did the same for our son, starting from the moment he could walk and talk. He, like our daughter, had to learn our family values and what was expected of him.

I'm sure, if you have children, you can identify with this. So much love gets poured onto our children. We want the best for them. We want to be proud of them. We want to see them happy and living meaningful lives. And yes, we want them to appreciate what we've done for them. We all desire a good relationship with our children, whether they're small or grown.

How could the God who created us in His image be any different? He also loves His children only not with the flawed love we humans have but with a perfect love. Jesus told us as much when he said, "If you then, being evil, know how to give good gifts to your children, how much more will your Father who is in heaven give good things to those who ask Him!"[1]

We have been adopted by a loving God who will nurture and grow us into the kind of people He can be proud of. We have the best, wisest parent, not simply in the whole world, but in the entire universe. Our heavenly Father is incomparable. As followers of Christ and children of God we have a family name unique and different than the rest of the world. Our surname is Christian, and that carries with it both benefits and responsibilities. Let's talk first about the behavior expected of us as adopted children of the Most High God.

In Psalm 23:3, David acknowledges that "...He guides me in paths of righteousness for his name's sake..."[2] Of course, our Creator wants us to live righteous lives so we can reap the benefits of that righteousness, but there is a bigger picture here. We are expected to live up to the name of the One who gave us life.

The Creator takes His name seriously, and we can find proof of this everywhere in Scripture. We especially see it when God is dealing with His people Israel, descendants of Abraham, Isaac and Jacob, the nation He chose to be His light in the world. Hear what He had to say to this people who wandered from Him and constantly had to be called back:

"Listen to this, O house of Jacob, you who are called by the name of Israel, and come from the line of Judah, you who take oaths in the name of the LORD and invoke the God of Israel – but not in truth or righteousness – you who call yourselves citizens of the holy city and rely on the God of Israel – the LORD Almighty is his name..." I am the LORD your God, who teaches you what is best for you, who directs you in the way you should go."[3]

Sheila translation: *You carry My Name. I expect you to live up to it and respect Me as Your father because I deserve your respect and I know what's best for you.*

Here God, himself, is reminding people just who He is. He is that powerful Being who defies description, that Being so great we are almost at a loss for words beyond saying He is.

God could have decided this was not a people worth bothering with and wiped the entire nation off the face of the earth. Think of how many of those ancient peoples we read about in the Bible who no longer exist. God could have done the same with the nation of Israel. But to stay true to His own name, He didn't. He constantly forgave His people.

He does the same with us, the new members of the family. I'm sure you've heard the saying, Thank God He doesn't give me what I really deserve. How true those words are!

It's great that God is so patient and forgiving, but we never want to take advantage of His mercy. We want to honor our Father, not be an embarrassment to Him.

Just as our children's behavior, good or bad, reflects on us as parents, so our behavior reflects on our heavenly Father and our Lord, Jesus. People are always watching, always ready to criticize, always willing to point out where we've gone wrong. Remember poor Job and his so-called helpful friends? They were quick to jump to conclusions.

People in our time are no different now. They rush to judgement, especially when it comes to those who follow Christ. I'm sure you can think of times in your own life when people either called you on your hypocritical behavior or made observations about the un-Christian behavior of other Christians.

I sure don't want to be "that kid," God's problem child, the talk of the neighborhood, the one who doesn't honor the family name. I bet you don't, either.

When we dishonor Him, God has every right to be angry. Read the anger behind God's scold in Jeremiah 7:9-11:

"Will you steal and murder, commit adultery and perjury, burn incense to Baal and follow other gods you have not known, and then come and stand before me in this house, which bears my Name, and say, 'We are safe' – safe to do all these detestable things? Has this house, which bears my Name become a den of robbers to you? But I have been watching! Declares the LORD."[4]

The temple was dedicated to God, it was where His people came to worship. What an insult to His name when His people didn't behave like they even knew Him and then showed up to offer lip service. *There. Made it to the temple. Got that checked off the list.*

✳ God went on to say, "For my own name's sake I delay my

wrath; for the sake of my praise, I hold it back from you, so as not to cut you off."[5]

In other words, because of who God was and because of His reputation as a powerful yet merciful God, He wasn't going to wipe out His people. Because He had made a covenant with the nation of Israel God would be true to His word, even when they veered away from Him.

If that doesn't prove what an amazing God we have I don't know what does. Think of the many times His people disappointed Him, the many times we still do. Yet, because of who He is and for His name's sake He will forgive. The human race has committed sin after sin, atrocity after atrocity down through the centuries, yet He is still willing to extend mercy to those who ask for it. Only the highest, noblest Being could do such a thing. I don't know about you, but if I were God, we'd have all been toast long ago.

To bring this closer to home, think of the child who ignores the parents all year long, who chooses to adopt values and a lifestyle that is an insult to them but sends a card on Mother's Day and Father's Day. Everyone – Mom, Dad, and kid, know that this is just a checklist item. There's no heart involved.

We certainly don't want to do that to our heavenly Father. We don't want to put in an appearance at church on Christmas and Easter and then live apart from our God the rest of the year. We don't want to read a chapter in our Bible, then mentally check that off as done and carry on with our bad attitudes. This is not the way to make our heavenly Father proud.

Psalm 29:2 tells us to ascribe to the Lord the glory due His name. Do we show the proper reverence to our God, both in and out of church? Do we acknowledge publicly when He's worked in our lives? Do we live lives that honor Him? The changes God makes in our hearts will show in our lives.

Proverbs 22:1 tells us that a good name is more important

than riches. That is a high value, indeed! Why is a good name so valuable? First of all, because it honors God. A good name also allows us to live a good life. How often over the years have you heard different companies refer to their company name as one you can trust? Trust is what makes human relations work, whether in business or in our personal lives. A good name goes hand in hand with a good life. That good name is what God wants for us and what we need to want for ourselves. The only way to earn it is by living a life that deserves it.

The New Testament is filled with admonishments to the early church to live exemplary lives and get along with each other. Not just for the sake of getting along but because others were watching. As Christians we live in a fishbowl.

Of course, we know this. We all shrink back from the idea of murder and adultery, robbing banks, physically attacking people, drunkenness. But it's not always those big-ticket sin items that get us in trouble.

In Song of Solomon 2:15, the writer talks about capturing the little foxes that destroy the vines. This, I learned, was a real problem in an agrarian society.[6] Foxes are primarily carnivores, preying on mice, rabbits, and birds, but it appears they have a taste for fruit as well, especially grapes. This was obviously a problem in Israel. Those foxes would bite off new shoots from the vine and chew away the roots. Sometimes they even enjoyed a grape or two. At the expense of the owner of the vineyard. A little nibble here, a little nibble there and pretty soon the whole crop would be lost.

It's like that with us as believers. Sometimes those little foxes get in and start nibbling away at what should be spiritually fruitful lives. When that happens, the name of Jesus Christ is not honored.

What are some of those little foxes?

How about gossip? (Yes, that again.) Often disguised as

concerned sharing or a prayer request. "We really need to pray for Esmerelda. She's _____." (Fill in the blank.)

Remember, what we say paints a picture of that other person, and gossip never paints a pretty one. It doesn't paint a pretty one of us, either.

And listening is as bad as speaking, for when we listen to gossip, we're not only encouraging the gossiper, but we're also bringing out the ugly side of ourselves, hoping for some titillating bit of news. In this modern age of technology, we have other means of entertainment. We don't need to be vicariously enjoying the mistakes and problems of others.

Grumbling is another poor use of verbal energy. If you want to see where grumbling gets you, go back to Exodus and read about the young nation of Israel and see where their constant grumbling got them.[7]

We often excuse our grumbling by saying, "I'm not grumbling about God. I'm grumbling about... my job, my boss, my coach, my teacher. You name it. But ultimately, that grumbling really is about God. We are letting Him know that we are not happy with how He is or isn't working in our life. The irony in this is that often the one to blame for the mess we are in is ourselves.

I challenge you to read Galatians 5:23 and then tell me where you see bad attitude listed as a fruit of the Spirit. Of course, you won't find it. Why? Because grumbling is a byproduct of discontent and discontent springs from an ungrateful and untrusting heart.

We've probably all done our share of grumbling, I'm sure. I know I have. But that is a habit I continue to work hard to kick. I've found that the best way to uproot ingratitude and grumbling is by focusing on God's goodness. What do you focus on, the bad things in your life or the good?

Do you have a home? Do you have food on the table? Do

you have someone in your life who cares for you? Are there agencies that exist to help people in need that you can take advantage of when you're struggling? How about health? Are you a cancer survivor? Maybe you've gone all your life and never had a serious disease. Did you see a beautiful sunrise or sunset this week? Get a chance to enjoy a cookie or a piece of chocolate? There is always something for which we can be grateful.

Even if you're in a place where you're having a hard time thinking of anything to be grateful for, remember God sent His Son to die for you and you have an amazing life waiting for you in the next world. You have been freed from the judgement of death that comes from sin. If we had nothing else to thank God for that, alone, would be enough.

Living up to the name of Christian in the truest sense of the word takes time and discipline, and it starts in our hearts and minds. As the saying goes, attitude is everything.

But boy, is it easy to tinker with our attitude! Let's look at some more areas where we tend to do this, some more of those little foxes.

How about stealing? Not the bank robbery kind but the more ordinary variety, such as taking income tax deductions that you really shouldn't be taking. Was that item you just put on your business charge card truly a legitimate deduction? If you're given too much money back from the grocery store checker, do you give it back or do you keep it and consider it found money? How about a bank error in your favor?

Little cheats are as visible to others as big cheats. An old friend used to be the king of little cheat. He was a believer and generous man. He loved the Lord. But he also loved to put one over on Uncle Sam whenever he could. He was a wheeler dealer, especially when it came to cars and motorcycles, and he concocted a system to save on sales tax when selling a vehicle.

He would say to the person he bought a vehicle from, "I will give you $800 as a gift (which is not taxable) and we'll say I bought this for $200. That way I'll only have to pay sales tax on two-hundred dollars."

Haha. That showed greedy Uncle Sam. It also showed a slippage of morals. This was the behavior of a Jacob the trickster, not the Israel God was calling this man to be.

You may be thinking, I would never do that. Yeah, me either.

But what about taking a job that pays "under the table" or not declaring tips?

Here's another little fox: driving over the speed limit. *It's only a few miles over.* Says Sheila Lead Foot. (Uh-oh, there's a name I don't want. But I sure seem to want to earn it!) On and on the rationalizing goes. *We shouldn't have to go so slow on this road. Nobody's around, for crying out loud.*

Except for maybe your children in the back seat. The baby fishes, watching Mommy and Daddy in the fishbowl, swimming as fast as they want because the rules don't apply to them. They watch Mommy and Daddy argue, too, and are all ears when their parents call each other unkind names.

Lack of loyalty hurts our spouses and dishonors God. Men who would never commit adultery may sneak down to the basement at night and bring up pornography on their computer, rationalizing that they aren't cheating on their wives. It's easy to forget Jesus' words in Matthew 5:27, 28: "You have heard that it was said, 'Do not commit adultery.' But I tell you that anyone who looks at a woman lustfully has already committed adultery with her in his heart."[8]

Likewise, we women think we're okay having a close relationship with a man not our husband as long as we don't sleep together. Ladies, if you've longed for this person, become emotionally attached to this person, you're as guilty as if you had. We euphemistically label this an emotional affair, but it's really adultery.

And how about loyalty in the workplace? In our friendships? Can people count on us once we've committed to something or do we have a reputation of being a shirker, of not following through with assigned tasks? Do we work to benefit the team or only ourselves? Do we do what's right or what's expedient?

The world watches. The world judges. Thankfully, for us, the ultimate Judge forgives. But this is behavior we need to stop because it dishonors our heavenly family name.

Here's something people who don't know God really love getting a ringside seat to watch – a church split. Arguments happen. They happened even in the early church, but this wasn't the vision God had for His people.

Jesus told His disciples, "By this all people will know that you are my disciples, if you have love for one another."[9] One of the earmarks of the early church was the love the believers had for each other, how they looked out for each other. In Acts 4:32-34 we read that they shared everything they had, many selling houses and lands and giving the money to the church so no one would be in need. Quite a testimony!

I have a friend who's an atheist. She once observed how great it was that Christians watched out for each other and took each other meals when one of them was sick. She half wished she was a Christian simply so she could experience that kind of generosity. I'm hoping one of these days she will make that commitment and be able to enjoy the benefits of life in God's family. Meanwhile, though, she's observing. Isn't it great that she's seeing good things!

It is a testimony of a very different matter when unbelievers see us at our worst. Years ago, my husband and I were caught in the middle of a church split. Looking back, it was hard to point to the exact stick of dynamite that blew things up. It was a many-headed monster and involved a lot of angry people, all angry for various reasons, wanting the pastor's head on a platter.

Those who were not happy began to look for supporters, and soon everyone was taking sides and we had a war on our hands. At the last contentious church business meeting in the church sanctuary the pastor called for everyone to stop the fighting and pray and one of the elders pointed a finger at him and said, "We're not going to pray. We're going to settle this right now."

Settle it we did. Half the church members left, swooping out the door in discontent. Faster than you could say, "Father, forgive us," the whole community knew what had happened. We were the church of the contentious. Unbelievers loved it. *See? Told you that whole Christianity thing is a crock.*

What would have happened if we'd committed to praying, to nobody leaving that sanctuary until forgiveness had been extended? We'll never know because we didn't opt to do that. To this day, I wish we had.

All this is not to say, if you are a Christian and you believe your church is wandering into the territory of heresy, that you're bound to stay and be part of that. If you take a stand on certain moral issues and your church doesn't you do not need to stay with that group. In fact, to stay is to approve. Leave, find a new church.

If you don't happen to be able to appreciate it when your church goes in a different direction regarding worship style or the handling of finances you are free to bid a fond farewell and worship with a different part of the body of believers who are gathering on a different block. No one needs to get mad at you if you crave a more liturgical worship service or if you're looking for more contemporary music. We all remain part of the body of Christ, no matter what corner we happen to meet on.

What we don't get to do is squabble over what music is being played or what color was chosen for the new carpet in the sanctuary. We don't get to nurse grudges and feed anger. We ask forgiveness when we've hurt someone and we extend it to those who have hurt us.

And we don't start a war. If we were allowed to war with each other Jesus wouldn't have rebuked Peter for cutting off the ear of the high priest's servant when the soldiers came to arrest Him. We take our stand on Scripture, we pray for those who we feel are in error. If asked, we share our Biblical reasons for leaving, but we depart in love and with grace.

Always, always we keep in mind Paul's admonition: "Be completely humble and gentle; be patient, bearing with one another in love. Make every effort to keep the unity of the Spirit through the bond of peace."[10] This is how we honor the name of Jesus our Lord. This is how we please our heavenly Father.

What are some practical ways we can apply this?

1. Be mindful of our attitudes

It is so easy to get our feelings hurt. *I didn't get picked to be on the worship team... Someone else was asked to head up the children's ministry... The church board cut my salary.*

Hurts are real, but the health and well-being of the body of Christ is more important than our individual hurt feelings. So when we've been hurt, we don't tell anyone and everyone who will listen. We cry out to our heavenly Father and ask Him for wisdom on how to deal with the situation. We go to the person who hurt us and try to work things out. We follow the instructions given in Matthew 18 and try to make peace with the person. If that doesn't work, then we bring along someone to help negotiate a peaceful outcome. Always, we ask God to heal our hurts and help us to show His love.

When someone has offended you, you might want to ask yourself the following questions? Am I looking for deliberate hurt where none was intended? How would Jesus want me to react to this? What reaction on my part will bring glory to His name?

1. Pray Before Behaving

When you find yourself in a situation where you are getting angry, before reacting give yourself a spiritual time out and ask God's guidance. This can be especially helpful when dealing with family. It's okay to say, "I need to process what just happened."

If you perceive you may be headed into a situation where conflict will arise, pray ahead of time, ask God for wisdom before attending that meeting or making that difficult phone call.

1. Honor That Gift

Jesus told a parable about a master leaving town and entrusting his property to his servants. All three were given talents (money) according to their ability. Two out of the three were diligent and did something with what they were given. Servant Number Three did nothing. His excuse? The master was a hard man and "I was afraid."[11]

Interesting. The other two servants weren't afraid. Why was that? I think it's because they knew they had nothing to fear. They loved the master and they wanted to please him. Number Three, not so much.

Granted, he was given the least responsibility of all.

Perhaps he didn't have the abilities the other two had. Possibly he hadn't done much to earn the master's trust. But he had still been entrusted with something. He still was offered a chance to serve his master and, when the master returned, be praised for a job well done.

The other two servants who got busy on their master's behalf received his praise and were rewarded when he returned while the other one missed out completely. Not only that, but he also received a humiliating scolding. Why? Because he'd dishonored the master and failed to appreciate what he'd been entrusted with.

We are the same as those servants. We all have varying abilities; we've all been given different gifts and each of us is expected to do something with the gift God has given us. When we scorn our gifts, we scorn our Lord and dishonor His name. When we honor and exercise our gifts, we honor Him.

No one is useless in God's kingdom. Whatever you're called to do, do it and know that big or small, you have a talent and God expects you to do something with it. There will come a day, if not in this life, then in the next, where you can bask in the satisfaction of knowing that you did as you were asked. There will come a time when the Master will say, "Well done, good and faithful servant! You have been faithful with a few things; I will put you in charge of many things. Come and share your master's happiness!"[12]

1. Do Good

Not only does this benefit the person or people to whom we're doing something good, it also benefits us by growing our character. In his letter to the Galatians Paul said, "Let us not become weary in doing good, for at the proper time we will reap a harvest if we do not give up. Therefore, as we have opportunity, let us do good to all, especially to those who are of the household of faith."[13] When we plant kindness, we reap joy and satisfaction.

More than that, we honor our Lord. Again, quoting Paul, this time his letter to the Colossian church: "And whatever you do, whether in word or deed, do it all in the name of the Lord Jesus, giving thanks to God the Father through him."[14]

Always, always, our lives are to point to Jesus. When we do good to others, we do good to Him. Remember Jesus' parable of the sheep and the goats? You can find it in Matthew 26. In it He talks about those blessed of God who would receive a wonderful inheritance in the kingdom, ones who saw the King hungry and fed him, who saw Him thirsty and gave him something to drink, who took him in as a stranger, gave him clothes, looked after him when he was sick and visited him in prison. "When did we do this?" asked the heirs to the kingdom, and he replied, "... I tell you the truth, whatever you did for one of the least of these brothers of mine, you did for me."[15]

Those kindnesses we do for others in the name of Jesus we do in His name and for Him. Our good behavior honors Him. Our kindness and generosity points to His kingdom.

But what if no one sees what we do? That is totally irrelevant. People will see what God wishes to reveal. There's no need to broadcast your good deeds. Do them quietly. What needs to be seen as a witness to God will be seen. What is done in secret will be rewarded by God, Himself.[16]

The name we operate under makes us ambassadors for the world yet unseen. Think of the responsibility. But also, think of the honor. What a great name we represent!

1. Matthew 7:11, New King James Version
2. New International Version

3. Isaiah 48: 1,2, 17b, New International Version
4. New International Version
5. Isaiah 48:9, New International Version
6. https://biblehelpsinc.org/publication/a-warfare-with-little-foxes
7. You can find instances of grumbling in Exodus 15:22-24, Numbers 14:1-4 and Numbers 21:4,5
8. New International Version
9. John 13:35, English Standard Version
10. Ephesians 4: 2,3 New International Version
11. Matthew 25: 24, 25
12. Matthew 25: 23, New International Version
13. Galatians 6:10, New International Version
14. Colossians 3:17, New International Version
15. Matthew 25:40, New International Version
16. Matthew 6: 1-6

TEN
WOMEN WHO OVERCAME A NAME

There are so many harsh names out there, so many unkind and unfair labels just waiting to attach themselves to us! Sometimes it might feel like no one else is going through what you're going through, no one else has been called the names you've been called or hurt the way you've been hurt. But there are women who have suffered what you are suffering. There are women who have been both physically and verbally abused. There are women who have suffered at the hands of others doing their best to hurt and belittle them. There are women who have also been wounded by well-intentioned remarks. So you are not alone.

I want to share here a few stories of women I interviewed who have been able to shake off those belittling names and negative labels. These women have turned negatives into positives, have re-adjusted their focus to see who they really are and who they're meant to be. They've walked away from the old and stepped into the new and are living their best lives. I hope their stories, which they kindly shared with me, will encourage you.

Catrina

Catrina was born with cerebral palsy in 1965. "They didn't know much back then," she told me. "I wasn't' supposed to live, but I did. I wasn't supposed to walk but I did at the age of two. I wore braces from my hips to the inside of my shoes until I was seven." The doctors treating her decided the braces weren't helping so the treatment was stopped. Stopping the treatment caused fallout. Catrina twists when she walks, and her left foot turns inward.

She told me she was teased a lot as a child, and when she was in the fourth grade a band of bullies beat her for simply being different. After that her, her stepfather moved the family from the city to the country, figuring she would be safer. There she found new bullies, who nicknamed her Weeble Wobbles.

Happily for Catrina, one of the popular boys at school championed her and taught her to stand up for herself. "From that day forward, I did whatever I wanted even if the way I did something stood out because I wasn't going to let my disability stop me," she told me.

And she didn't. She learned to ride a bike, got her driver's license when she turned eighteen and then got a job in an office doing accounting. The job was hard won and came after many potential employers looked at her "like I was an alien wanting a job." She never gave up, however, because she wanted her independence.

In spite of her challenges Catrina has been able to build a good life for herself. Now, at fifty-five, she's happily married with a thirty-two-year-old son and two granddaughters. "I still get people who point and whisper when I walk by them," she told me, "but I can walk by with my head held high."

I think if I were in her place, I would have a hard time not feeling bitter or getting frustrated, but Catrina doesn't let her condition get her down. "I fell blessed to be able to walk," she told me. Wow!

I suggested to Catrina that she is a true overcomer and that should be here name. "I love to be called Overcomer," she responded. "But in reality, we all overcome something in our lives."

This response shows such a humble practicality. Catrina could have named herself Mara and turned bitter, seeing nothing but the bad in her life. Instead, she has triumphed over a horrible disability.

Maybe, like her, you have a physical handicap to overcome. I hope Catrina's story inspires you.

Audrey

"I grew up with abuse of all kinds at home, in school, and by my husband," Audrey told me. One of the first experiences she remembers is of being harassed in the girls' bathroom at school. She was not quite ten when she started menstruating and the senior class girls greatly enjoyed themselves looking under and over the bathroom stall, offering taunts. She found no comfort at home when her mother called her a whore. Her father, angry with her when she rebelled over doing the dishes, banged her head on the kitchen cabinet doors. She was raped when she was eleven and then again when she was sixteen and once more when she was twenty-two.

She escaped her horrible home environment only to find herself married to an alcoholic husband who became both verbally and physically abusive when he was drunk. This set the example for her two boys, who grew to also be abusive.

Surely, after all this, Audrey would be both bitter and vengeful. Instead, she is clinging to God. "God is the only thing keeping me alive," she told me.

My mouth dropped when told me that she has forgiven

everyone who treated her so horribly. How on earth could she forgive so may so much?

"I left it to God to deal with my abusers," she said.

What a wise decision! And God surely will. Being able to forgive those who have hurt her so terribly will enable her to move forward, and I pray that Audrey will come into her own and become all that God intended for her to be. Here is another woman who surely has earned the name Overcomer.

Debbie

Debbie was raised in an Italian family where, she told me, sharing food was how they showed love. "Not surprisingly, I began to get chubby in my childhood." I bet a lot of us can relate to that!

She went on to tell me that when she was thirteen when her parents divorced because her father fell in love with another woman. It was later implied to her that her mother's weight problem may have contributed to her father's dissatisfaction with the marriage. *Oh, boy*, I thought as I read what she'd written to me, *I can almost see where we're going.*

Sure enough, as Debbie got older and struggled with weight issues, concerns with how that would affect her relationships began to show up. "I did not realize it, but I had an undiagnosed condition called PCOS and insulin resistance, so managing my weight as a teenager became very difficult for me, and I began trying to diet. Once, a crush named Louie told my friend that he might have considered going out with me if I lost weight. A male friend at school told mutual friends that if I lost weight, I would be one of the prettiest girls at school. They probably thought they were being complimentary, but hearing these things only added to my low self-esteem."

Debbie went on to talk about how hard she exercised to lose weight. In her senior year she lost thirty-five pounds, going down from 195 to 160. That was when she met her first boyfriend. He, himself was a little overweight, but she didn't care.

His mother, however, wasn't so generous. Mom made it plain she didn't approve of Debbie. When Debbie hypothesized that Mom probably thought her son should date a thinner girl the boyfriend didn't disagree. Needless to say, that relationship did not last.

Debbie continued her story, talking about the guy she dated who was impressed by her ordering a glass of ice to chew on when they went through a MacDonald's drive-in and then promising to take her shopping for new pants if she'd lose another thirty-five pounds.

Perhaps you're reading this and seeing similarities to your own past experiences. If so, let me just say that I'm sorry. Both for what you went through and for my own attitudes as I look back on my high school days. I had a best friend who was extremely obese, and I can remember trying to inspire her to lose weight in the most unhelpful ways. Even the best-intentioned words can be hurtful, and we need to choose carefully and prayerfully before speaking. And sometimes we need to stay silent.

Debbie's story has a happy ending. She met the love of her life who accepted her as she was. "Throughout our courtship I constantly put myself down and said I was fat. He would never allow that. He told me and showed me over and over again that he loved me, that my body was beautiful and that he was attracted to me. Throughout our marriage we both became very heavy, and I worried that he would find someone else like my father had, but his unconditional love for me never wavered." How is that for true love!

You might be thinking, *Well, he wasn't so perfect himself so who was he to say anything?* To that I will reply I've heard many tales over the years of men who weren't so physically perfect themselves who still expected their wives to be. The double standard is alive and well, and insults and cruel words hurt no matter who delivers them.

Debbie and her husband finally saw their weight gain as a health issue. (She was diagnosed with type 2 diabetes, and he had climbed to over 300 pounds.) They both underwent gastric sleeve surgery. Both of them are now working hard to stay healthy.

"Our love for each other is the main reason that I now feel good about myself and my body. I finally understand that I don't need to be perfect because I'm perfect for him," she concluded.

What a great happy ending to her story that Debbie is maintaining that temple for the Holy Spirit, but realizing that God doesn't expect her to be perfect. And kudos to her husband who has always seen how valuable she is as a person.

What name would you give Debbie? I hope she has named herself Beautiful.

Rachel

Rachel is another woman who had to learn to see herself as valuable just as she is. She told me, "I grew up in a family that was obsessed with physical beauty and being 'thin.' Growing up on Cocoa Beach in the 1980's only made me more self-conscious. I have a short, stocky body with a lot of muscle mass for a woman. I will never be tall, slender, and delicate ... the only acceptable qualities in my family. My value or lack thereof has always been directly related to my weight."

It wasn't until Rachel met her husband, married and had a child that her life lens changed. It started with a phone lecture from her father after she had her first baby. Her father told her she needed to make sure she was keeping her weight in check and that she also needed make sure she always had her makeup on when he husband came home from work.

She hung up and fell apart. "I was a new mom in a new town with no friends, and the one adult I had talked to all day made me feel like a fat loser who could not turn my husband's head," she remembered.

Her husband came home and found her sitting on the floor crying. He picked her up, kissed her and said, "If I wanted to hug a 2X4 I would go sleep in a lumber yard! Rachel, you are exactly as you should be, and I just want you to be healthy." Ah, that every man would say kind words like this to his wife when she's feeling like she doesn't measure up. This, Rachel said, was when she learned that her value was not connected to her dress size.

I asked her where God fit into this. "Not directly," she said. "It was more of us truly understanding our Christian marriage vows and what it means to be a godly person. When you look at each other as a gift from God just for you, it changes the lens through which you see life."

So perhaps when we look at ourselves, when we look at each other, we need to make sure we're looking through the right lens.

Judith

Judith told me that she grew up in a very dysfunctional household with an alcoholic, sometimes violent father and mostly absent mother. She was the oldest child and had to take on many adult responsibilities.

"My father loved me in his own way but called me Mouthy because I was often angry and talked back," she said.

I suspect the tone of voice that went with the name calling was hardly amused or tolerant. And I bet much of her anger was understandable.

I love what Judith told me next. "I decided to embrace it –

became a prosecutor, public speaker, and law school professor. Just try shutting me up now!"

Judith was able to turn an insult into a challenge and a challenge into an inspiration. She has made good use of the gifts God gave her.

Mary

Mary got teased in school, not because she was overweight, but because she was busty. "In junior high two students, one a guy, the other a gal decided to call me Bubbles," she remembered. "They tormented me by whispering it as I passed them in the hall or in the lunchroom. I felt very self-conscious and ugly. Add to this a brother who also loved to tease me, and life was horribly difficult."

I can imagine. Hard enough to get teased over something you're sensitive about and have no control over by outsiders. It shouldn't happen at home, which is supposed to be a safe place.

"The bright spot in all of this was the fact that I had an intimate relationship with God," Mary continued. "I would talk to Him about these people who tormented me and read Psalms 13 where David says that he felt abandoned by God because David's enemy was exalted over him. Finally, he stated, 'But I have trusted in your lovingkindness; my heart shall rejoice in your salvation. I will sing to the Lord, because He has dealt bountifully with me.'* I had to focus on what God could do and not on myself. I needed to realize that God would care for me and take care of them."

He did. Sadly, the life of neither of Mary's tormentors ended well. Mary, on the other hand, married, had a family, and has lived joyfully ever after. She's a leader in her church and has been mom to many people in need over the years.

As for her brother, he hasn't changed. But she told me, "I am able to ignore my brother's jibes because I know God has a great deal to say about me and it's all loving."

Maybe we can all learn from that last statement of Mary's. Instead of focusing on the bad things others have to say about us, let's focus on what our heavenly Father has to say.

Lauri

As I read Lauri's story, I saw her falling into the same trap I had. Name-calling led her to see herself as ugly. It all started with a haircut in eighth grade. A friend offered to cut her hair so it would look like the one on a model in a magazine they were looking at. The friend got carried away, just about buzz-cutting her hair around the ears.

Mom to the rescue. Lauri's mother took her down the street to her friend who was a hair stylist. The stylist, after seeing the hair disaster, prescribed a pixie cut.

"But back then no one had a pixie cut," Lauri told me. "I hated it. I went to school the next day and the most popular boy in my school said I looked like a peacock. That became my name until the end of eighth grade. I was mortified and that is when I started being very self-conscious about my looks. I thought I was so ugly. It also began my quest to gain validation from others instead of myself, and especially from males. It led me to toxic relationships and abusive partners."

Look what one nickname did to a young girl. This is such a great reminder to us as mothers to make sure we are balancing the negativity out there with positive nicknames and encouragement.

Happily, Lauri didn't stay stuck on that negative track. "Something finally clicked, and I learned that it is not my responsibility to be appealing to men. The only person I try to impress is myself. It took a very long time, and I had a long road of hardships because of a simple nickname given over a haircut. Now I'm happily married with three handsome boys all under the age of five, I'm in the best shape of my life and thanks to many nights of hard work, conversations with the

Lord above (and a lot of crying to Him, too), I couldn't love myself more."

Yay Lauri! You are walking proof that we can pull off those negative names.

Martha

Martha suffered a stroke at the age of twenty-five in 1977. She had to learn how to talk again, and her left hand remained numb. To this day she says the palm of her hand still is numb.

She was supposed to go to physical therapy but only went once because her husband said she wasn't worth the money. Still, she tried to do things on her own that she'd been shown in that one therapy session at home and make her numb side work. She would stand in front of a mirror and practice saying words.

Speaking is still a struggle for her. She says, "I do pretty good, but when I am tired I start to slur my words and I have to think about every word I say."

Her husband constantly told her "No one wants to look at you. You are good for nothing." In spite of her handicap, she did her best to take care of the children and maintain a home while he was out drinking and seeing other women. He finally left her for another woman.

"And then my fight back to life really started," she said. Her husband had beaten her down so much that she was petrified to even walk into a store.

Here is another story of triumph. "One day I sat myself down and decided I couldn't live like that anymore. I got up and that started my rebirth," she told me. She went back to college and persisted even though she often had trouble retaining what she learned. After getting an education she went to work for Target and within three months was a department manager. Married again, she lives with her sister and husband and helps care for her sister's developmentally disabled son. "I fought my way back both mentally and physically and I guess I have done okay," she finished.

I guess she has! Martha's story is a great reminder that even though times turn hard it doesn't mean our story is over. With a handicap to overcome and a husband naming her Worthless she could have easily turned bitter against God for the awful things that happened to her. Instead, she climbed out of the pit of despair and allowed God to put her feet on higher ground.

"I have always thanked God for anything good that has come my way and have asked Him many times to help me make it through the day," she told me. Obviously, He has.

Jessica

I have known my friend Jessica for many years. Also a writer, she is as gifted as she is kind. However, her gifts weren't nurtured as a child. "Growing up as the daughter of a classy, but very needy, alcoholic mother, I was given several hurtful names," she told me. "Though I craved my mother's affection and affirmation, I was an easy target for her judgement and scathing criticism. For instance, I was chunky (and have battled weight issues all my life), so I received labels such as Fat Girl and Unacceptable. I was also good at my studies and at the top of my classes, but that was never appreciated. Mom saw me as competitive."

It was heartbreaking to hear Jessica's story unfold. Instead of encouraging her gifts and trying to help her in kindness and compassion her mother chose to see her though a negative lens. Of course, when you look at a person, determined to focus on what displeases you, that is all you will see. And isn't it often easier to see the other person's faults rather than your own, to point your finger in any direction other than yours.

Jessica kept trying to please her mother. The summer she turned twenty she cut short her summer jobs to help her mother move cross country after her mother's marriage ended.

Sadly, the sacrifice wasn't enough. The furniture movers were delayed weeks after their estimated delivery time and could give no definite arrival time. Jessica couldn't hang around indefinitely. She needed to get home and prepare for her junior year of college. Reasoning that her teenage brother could help their mother unpack, Jessica booked her return flight home. Her mother was furious.

"She unleashed a tirade of abuse that scorched my soul, physically backing me into the guest room. As I cowered in the corner, hands over my face, I began to sob uncontrollably. Still she continued to spew her rage as she exited the room. Slamming the door, she screamed, 'You are the scum of the earth!' Sunned and broken-hearted, I had once again fallen short of mom's expectations, and she lashed out at me with a vengeance."

When I read these words I envision this young woman, cowering before a huge, dark dragon, trying desperately to ward off flames of fire. Her mother never struck her. She didn't need to. The things she said inflicted damage that was much deeper.

But Jessica has been able to rise above the harsh treatment she received from her mother. "It took years for me to see myself as God saw me," she admitted. But she did come to see herself as her heavenly Father saw her. She did come to realize that she was not the scum of the earth, that she was "a precious daughter of the King raised by a damaged and hurting woman." Despite her many insecurities she came to discover that God loved her beyond measure.

"In fact," she told me, "He used the unconditional love of a humble and caring man to repair my damaged spirit. The best gift God ever gave me was a husband whose affirming words and servant's heart helped me to realize my worth as a person. Over the decades of our marriage, God has challenged me to not only receive Christ's love for me, but to extend forgiveness to those who hurt me. Over forty years have passed since that awful afternoon and the sting is gone. Now I know my real name! I am Beloved, and so grateful that God's love causes me to shine like the princess He created."

Charlene

Charlene is another dear friend and an inspiration. Over the years she has helped countless women struggling in abusive relationships. And she's well qualified.

Charlene's childhood was a struggle. Her father was an alcoholic who was abusive and kept his family living in fear. She believes he didn't feel good about himself and that spilled over into his dealings with everyone in his life. It certainly spilled onto her. He had pet names for her such as Crazy and Stupid.

Charlene says she knew deep down the labels of Stupid and Crazy were a lie because she was a good student in high school. She'd say to herself, "You can't be that crazy."

He decided she was though, when she became a Christian at the age of fourteen. Her dad couldn't stand the idea of having a Christian in the family. As far as he was concerned, they were all hypocrites.

Sadly, when she got married she learned she'd gone from one abuser to another. On the surface her husband came across as ideal. Perhaps if they'd dated longer before marrying, she'd have discovered he wasn't. But, Charlene explained, her church believed fast courtships were the best way to stave off pre-marital sex. It wasn't until they were married that she learned how controlling this new man in her life was. It started showing in small ways, the first being a temper tantrum he threw when friends started looking at their wedding pictures but not doing so in the order he'd assembled those pictures.

The marriage soon went far beyond temper tantrums and devolved into verbal and physical abuse and adultery. At one point, when she asked if she and the children could get out of the house and go somewhere he fetched his sawed-off shotgun and threated that if she said one more word about getting out of the house he'd blow her head off.

"These kinds of men come into a woman's life to destroy. They think that in abusing you that you will give up."

Charlene didn't give up. She hung in there. They had five children together.

But things didn't get better. Finally, they moved north. He found work in Brooklyn. She and the children stayed in a little house a long way from the city and with no car and no money, she was isolated. Meanwhile, her husband was enjoying himself with the girlfriend he'd found. Just to make sure she wouldn't get any ideas of leaving he'd tell her, "You're dumb, you're stupid, you're fat. Nobody else is going to want you. Nobody's going to marry you with five kids to take care of. I'm gonna get me a woman and move to Brooklyn and get me one of those townhouses. We'll be laying in bed, making love, and I'll be thinking of you there with all those kids. I will be single, and you'll have those kids and nobody will want you." That future girlfriend was already a real thing as he would be gone on weekends and spending money on her. If ever a man qualified for the role of villain, it was this man.

But God saw what Charlene was going through and sent a messenger to encourage her. One day she made the trip to the Department of Social and Health Services to see if she could get food stamps. While she was there a short, little man walked in, singing gospel songs. Her walked up to Charlene and said, "I have a message for you from God. You come and see me before you leave."

I think I'd have been unnerved by such an announcement and run the other way, but Charlene did end up talking to the man. His message for her? "What you are going through with you husband, whether that man be living, whether he be dead or whether he be gone, God is going to grant you peace."

Two weeks later she found that peace when she went to a church with her husband's aunt, who had been trying hard to talk him into changing his ways. During that service the pastor had a special word of advice for her. He said, "Whatever is holding you down I want you to call it out when go under the water. God is going to set you free." When she came up, she knew she was free. She was not the same person.

Two weeks later she heard God whisper, "Go home, go South." She saved a little bit of government assistance money she'd gotten and bought bus tickets home for herself and her children. Once back home in Georgia God provided a place for her and her children to stay – an older woman living alone in a big house invited them to come live with her.

As God continued to provide for Charlene and her family, she came to realize that she was loved and valuable. It wasn't instant. Charlene told me it took her five years to get to know God as her father.

Since then, she's come a long way. The abusive men in her life are history and she is married to a kind, godly man. They've been married almost thirty-two years. For the last twenty years she has been an advocate for abused women both through the church and in the workplace. She's taken women into her home, led support groups, and worked in shelters. She is currently working as a community resource advocate.

Charlene now refers to herself as the woman who God has called for a purpose and for His season. She is beloved by many, and I see her as a woman who knows her worth in God. I find it interesting to see that she came full circle from being told she was less to being someone who has accomplished so much, from being told that no one would want her to becoming a woman dearly loved and depended upon by so many. Charlene is proof that you don't have to live up to the negative names people call you.

Monica

Writing is a tough business. I always say that every writer pays her dues somewhere along the way. Monica is a Christian writer who really paid her dues, but not just as a writer. She also paid for her faith. Sadly, as her faith in Christ grew her marriage disintegrated and what she dubbed as seven years of emotional abuse and turmoil ended in divorce. It was time for a new beginning.

"Finally, in June 2008, after a book signing in Oklahoma City, Oklahoma, I flew home to North Carolina, resolute in being single to pursue my faith freely," she told me. "I began working on a novel shortly after about a woman healing from a divorce herself, talented in so many aspects but languishing in finding her own path... So much of what I was experiencing went into my book that the lines blurred between reality and fiction. The book ended happily; my own life at the time not so much." It was her first foray into writing romantic suspense, and she told me that friends and relatives kept telling her she needed to include more sex in her books so they'd sell better. "I'd smile at them, knowing the biblical principles that guided my everyday life were going to be in my books."

Her novel, *Kissing Hollywood*, received a starred review in *Publisher's Weekly*, which is huge validation for an author. The book was selling well and authors she admired and respected were saying great things to their followers about it. Life was great.

Until she began to get disparaging reviews on various websites, including Amazon. Then the name calling began: Bible Thumper, Smug Christian, Unrealistic Believer. Bad reviews are painful for writers. Name calling – I can imagine how devastating that was. "I took the reviews personally.

Hateful comments referencing scenes in my book about faith sent me into a sorrowful place," she shared.

Perhaps you, also have been insulted or called names because of your faith. If so, you have been blessed. And name calling is nothing compared to what Christians in other parts of the word endure. For many, their faith costs them their lives. The apostle Paul talks about sharing in the fellowship of Christ's suffering in Philippians 3:10 and in John 15:18-27 we see Jesus cautioning his disciples that they wouldn't be winning any popularity contests as his followers. Far from it! Just as Jesus was hated by many, they would be also.

Nothing has changed. The fallen world hates God and especially hates Christians. We are the world's party poopers, always shaking fingers and talking about right and wrong. Darkness detests the light. But to bear the name Christian is an honor and all who suffer for their beliefs will, in the end, be rewarded.

How did Monica survive this? "I didn't remain in a place of defeat," she said. "I thought of Jesus and how He was chided, openly mocked and scorned, and I held my chin up..." I love Monica's final advice: "Just because the world doesn't openly accept what you're giving, give it anyway. There are those waiting to receive your gifts as only you can give. Be true to who God made you."

What great words for us to remember!

THE STORIES of all these women share something in common. They came to see their worth. They all experienced hardship and hurt. They were all told that they were of little value, that they were unworthy of kindness and respect. And yet, they conquered those bad labels and claimed their true identity as valuable women.

I love Jessica's words: "Now I know my real name!"

Do you?

*PSALM 13:5, 6, New American Standard Bible

ELEVEN
REMEMBERING WHO I AM

Sometimes we forget who we are in Christ. It's also easy to forget Who our God is and what He is capable of doing in, through and for us. The hurries and worries of everyday life rush in and swamp us. That mountain top experience we had gets lost in the mist. Trouble comes and, like Naomi, we decide that God has dealt bitterly with us. It's easy to lose track of the name that is rightfully ours as His children.

How can we keep sight of the people we've been called to be? How can we remember the new name the Lord gave us?

Let me give you a few suggestions that might help.

1. Keep Your Eyes Open

I love reading about Abraham's encounter with heavenly visitors in Genesis 18. We're told that he was just sitting in front of his tent enjoying the day when he looked up and saw three men standing nearby. Scholars think two of the men were angels. The third? Possibly the Lord, Himself, a pre-incarnate visit. The key words in the beginning of this story are "looked up." Having already experienced the presence of God, he was open to seeing what was right in front of his eyes. Are you?

It's easy to miss God's hand at work in our lives, especially if we aren't watching for it. Be on the lookout! As you come to see who you are in Christ, dumping those old negative names, your vision will improve, and you'll start seeing yourself as God sees you. He will bring opportunities for you to live up to that new name. Watch for them. Be aware of those situations where you can exercise your trust, see yourself as worthy, and remind yourself that you're forgiven. God will bring opportunities for you to reap the joy that comes from living up to your new name.

Some of these situations will be tests, a chance for you to measure your progress. Whether you experience blessing or trial, be sure to ask God to help you see the situation through His eyes.

1. Remember Who God is

He is the God who sees. He is our provider. He is our banner. He is the great I Am. And He cares for us! When we remember the character of God this, too, helps open our eyes to see His hand at work in our lives.

That raise at work, for example. Don't see it simply as a reward for your diligence (although I'm sure you are being diligent in your workplace). Instead, see it as God moving on your behalf. That job loss? Remind yourself that God is your provider. Here is your opportunity to trust Him to live up to His name and provide. Maybe God is calling you to step out in faith and move a new direction, trusting Him to guide you. Take the step. Be bold and courageous.

Trial or sorrow, reward, or joy – our heavenly Father sees everything we experience. He won't forsake us. If we take time to pray and to pay attention, we might just see that He is living up to His many names, doing something in us, changing us for the better and using us for His glory.

1. Jog Your Memory

• In Writing

IN PSALM103:2 we see King David the psalmist reminding himself not to forget the benefits of belonging to God. After that reminder he goes on to name what God has done for him.

We, like David, can remind ourselves of God's goodness to us, can remind ourselves that we are His and He loves us. There are different ways we can do this.

You might want to start a journal. You don't have to write in it every day, but record those times you see God's hand at work, the ways He's living up to His great name. When you have doubts about who you are, when those old names that no longer apply try to rear their ugly heads write down who you are in Christ and how God is revealing that to you. This can be immensely helpful, not only in the moment, but further down the road when you need a refresher course.

Of course, it's nice to be able to note all this in a fancy notebook with gilt edged pages, but a college-lined notebook will do just as well. Make note of answered prayers, healed relationships, triumphs over the temptation to be bitter or angry. Record both big blessings that encouraged you in your faith walk and small treats that gave you a lift when you were feeling down. Big and small, all blessings come from God and show that you matter to Him. Be sure and journal about the name you have as God's daughter and how you are living up to that name.

I'm very happy I journaled during my battle with uterine cancer. It kept me in God's Word and the Word embedded in my mind when I was fighting the disease. It helped me to remember my name, Sheila the Faithful. Journaling not only allowed me to note my fears and frustrations, but it also recorded the encouragement and insight I gained during this time. It's great to be able to read it now and remember how very real His presence was and to see how hanging in there with Him helped me.

I'm currently writing about different events taking place in my own small world and in the world around me, making note of my concerns, answers to prayer and thoughts on life in general. Maybe someday my children will benefit from reading about my spiritual journey. Maybe, if you start a journal, yours will as well.

- In Pictures

Journaling may not be your thing. You may find it a challenge simply writing emails. How about taking pictures? I have a collection of memories in my iPad photo file and on my phone, and every once in a while, I scroll through them. I have shots from trips my husband and I have enjoyed, the view from the balcony of our condo, some family pictures and even a picture of the daughter we lost, eyes closed, looking peaceful, wearing the special outfit we purchased for her to be buried in.

That one makes me cry. But it also reminds me that she is "sleeping" and when the Lord returns that sleeping body will be raised from the dead. I know I will see her again one day and she will be in a glorious, new body. I look at that picture, wipe my eyes, and tell myself, "She will have a new name and it will be something that reflects the new, imperishable, perfect her."

- With Memory Triggers

We often keep gifts people have given us or bring back souvenirs from trips we've taken. Perhaps you have a memento of some sort that reminds you of how God watched over you. Put it out where you can see it. Not only will it help you remember, but it will also give you an opening to talk about what God's done in your life.

I have a beautiful cross necklace. When I wear that I am making a statement to myself as well as others: I belong to Jesus Christ, and therefore I am an adopted daughter of the most high God. My spiritual surname is Christian.

Which brings us to one more suggestion for how we can remember who we are and Whose we are.

- In Conversation

Surely Abraham must have told his son Isaac how God appeared to him and gave him a promise and a new name. Surely, at some point, Jacob the cheater who became Israel must have told his story to his sons about his transforming experience since they and their offspring became the tribes of Israel.

If God has given you a new name and a new outlook, you owe it to the next generation, those who will follow after you to share the story of the way He has worked in your heart and is working in your life.

I love how Moses, in Deuteronomy 11:18,19, instructs the nation of Israel to pass on what God did for them to the next generation. "Fix these words of mine in your hearts and minds; tie them as symbols on your hands and bind them on your foreheads. Teach them to your children, talking about them when you sit at home and when you walk along the road, when you lie down and when you get up."

Let's not be afraid to tell others what God has done for us. In doing so, we testify to His greatness and honor His name. Every time we speak of it, we keep God's kindness to us fresh in our minds. And that helps us stay connected to Him, which, in turn, helps us to continue to grow into that good name He has given us.

1. Find an Accountability Partner

As I mentioned earlier, over the years I developed this habit of insulting myself when I do something stupid or forget or misunderstand something. One of my favorite phrases: What a dope. Or else I'll end a lament with the word, "Duh." Well, duh, how stupid is that!

My husband has started calling me on it every time I put myself down. "No name calling," he reminds me. "Remember what you wrote in your book."

Maybe you need to find an accountability buddy who point out when you slip and call yourself an unflattering and undeserved name or let someone's cruel teasing get to you, someone who will remind you who you are in Christ.

1. Resist Doubt

Sowing doubt is a spiritual tactic Satan has used since the dawn of human history. He first tried it on Eve in the garden of Eden with that famous phrase, "Has God really said?"[1] Satan still favors this tactic.

God has told you that you are of value. Satan will ask, "Does anyone really care how you feel... what you think... what you have to offer?" He might whisper, "You're old now. Your day is done," or "You're not qualified to do that," or "You don't have any skills or talent anyone can use."

Oh, please. If you're here, you are here for a reason and that reason is to glorify your heavenly Father. If He had nothing for you to do, you'd be gone.

God has forgiven you, but Satan will say, "Yes, but what about that one sin? That is unforgivable. You may as well pack it in. Get what you can out of this life because you're off the list for the next." Quote 1 John 1:9 to him. You have confessed your sins and God is faithful and just and has forgiven them. And cleansed you from that old unrighteousness!

And then, let's think about the temptation during trials and suffering to reclaim the name of Mara. "You have every right to be bitter," Satan will inform you. "Do you really think God cares about this? Look what He's letting you go through. Maybe He's abandoned you, given up on you."

That won't fly either. Remember, God has promised never to forsake us. We are precious to Him. Look what He allowed His beloved Son to go through so that you could be forgiven and have a glorious existence in the next life! Remember Naomi and how her story ended. Remember how God restored Job.

We will all go through trials. We will all suffer because that is what happens in this fallen world. But the Lord will not desert us. Think of the honor and glory that awaited Jesus after his death, after he rose from the dead. Think of eternity. Our troubles here and now are shorter than a blink. Our eternity is glorious. Meanwhile, here on earth, God may be testing you or refining you, turning your life to gold. He might be allowing you the opportunity in difficult circumstances to be an ambassador for Him to unbelievers around you. You may simply be dealing with the consequences of your own bad choices and living through a time of discipline.

Even if you're not sure why you are experiencing what you are, you can be sure of the fact that your heavenly Father has not given up on you. You may be having a hard time seeing that love, but it's there, all the same. Satan will often show up on your doorstep with a prettily wrapped gift of doubt and insecurity. Don't open the door.

When he insists, "You have every right to be bitter... fearful... angry at God," quote him Romans 8:28: "And we know that in all things God works for the good of those who love him, who have been called according to his purpose."[2] God will work out your circumstances in a way that fulfills the divine purpose He has for you. That includes both our sufferings and our mistakes.

And that whole new name thing? Satan will love to scoff at that. "Nothing but imagination and wishful thinking," he'll say. "God didn't really speak to you."

To that I say don't listen because he is a liar. If you have been praying, if you have been reading your Bible, and the Holy Spirit whispers, "God wants to give you a new name, God has something better in mind for you than that negative name you've given yourself or others have saddled on you," believe it. God is calling you to a closer walk and wants you to see yourself as forgiven and restored and has called you to glorify Him. Answer the call. Accept the name.

6. Honor the name.

Get used to it. Affirm it. You are:

A Child of God

Forgiven

Beloved

Valuable

Beautiful in God's Eyes

Provided For

Faithful in All Things

A New Creation

Always Improving

. . .

YOU HAVE:

A purpose

A future

A hope

A heavenly Father who ransomed you

A Savior who died for you and whose Spirit is working in you today

You are beloved and beautiful in God's eyes and redeemed for His purposes thanks to Jesus Christ. Whatever is in your past is in your past. You have the present in which to live the life God called you to. Whatever negative names you were once given do not apply to the new you. God has named you, His child. Appreciate that new name and walk in that new life.

And now you know exactly what's in a name. Rejoice in yours!

1. Genesis 3:1

2. New International Version

ABOUT THE NEW ME

Dear Beloved Daughter of God, I hope it has sunk soul deep how very loved you are and how very much God values you. You may feel you still have some growth ahead of you. If so, you might find the following questions a helpful personal reflection guide.

How have I failed to see myself as God sees me?

Is there a name I have taken on that conflicts with who I am as a daughter of God?

What new, better name might God have for me?

Scripture verses that speak to me:

Other ways God has spoken to me:

How might God be working in my life right now?

What gifts has God entrusted to me?

Where/how can I use those gifts?

Is there someone I have wronged?

Steps I Need to Take to repair that relationship:

Is there someone I have failed to forgive?

Scripture verses that will help me to forgive:

What names have I bestowed on others that I shouldn't have?

How I plan to change my behavior going forward:

Things I am thankful for:

Answers to prayer, ways that God has proved Himself faithful:

Further thoughts:

I hope you will revisit these questions as the need arises, remembering that we are all works of art ... in progress. God is continuing and will continue to make you into the woman He wants you to be because He loves you.

And Finally...

Take with you this reminder from Psalm 9:9. Here it is in the New International Version, one of my favorite Bible translations: "The Lord is a refuge for the oppressed, a stronghold in times of trouble. Those who know your name will trust in your, for you Lord, have never forsaken those who seek you."

When we know all that His name represents, we can trust Him. Wherever you are, whatever you've been through, whatever lies ahead, know that God is at work in your life, and you can, indeed, trust Him.

Made in United States
Orlando, FL
01 November 2024